THE ROAD TO NISSAN

INDUSTRIAL RELATIONS IN PRACTICE
General Editor: Jim Matthewman

Industrial Relations in Practice is a new series for personnel managers, union negotiators, employees, welfare advisers and lawyers. With an emphasis on current practice in leading British organisations and trade unions, the series takes an overall independent stance, with titles aimed at both sides of industry. The various authors, who have been selected from management, independent research groups and labour organisations, address themselves to topics of immediate and practical concern to the work-force of today and those responsible for its management.

Published titles

Edward Benson
A GUIDE TO REDUNDANCY LAW
THE LAW OF INDUSTRIAL CONFLICT

Alastair Evans and Stephen Palmer
NEGOTIATING SHORTER WORKING HOURS

Susan M. Shortland
MANAGING RELOCATION

Forthcoming titles

Gary Bowker
DISCRIMINATION AT WORK

Philip James
UNDERSTANDING SHOP STEWARDS

Susan Johnstone and James Hillage
CONTROLLING INDUSTRIAL ACTION

David Murray-Bruce
PROMOTING EMPLOYEE HEALTH

The Road to Nissan

Flexibility, Quality, Teamwork

Peter Wickens

Director of Personnel and Information Systems
Nissan Motor Manufacturing (UK) Ltd

MACMILLAN
PRESS

First edition 1987
Reprinted 1988 (five times), 1989 (twice)

Published by
THE MACMILLAN PRESS LTD
Houndmills, Basingstoke, Hampshire RG21 2XS
and London
Companies and representatives
throughout the world

Typeset by Footnote Graphics, Frome

Printed and Bound in Great Britain by
Billing and Sons Ltd
Worcester

British Library Cataloguing in Publication Data
Wickens, Peter
The road to Nissan: flexibility, quality,
teamwork.
1. International business enterprises—
Japan—Management
I. Title
658'.049'0952   HD62.4
ISBN 0–333–41919–7 (hardcover)
ISBN 0–333–45765–X (paperback)

To Helga, Tara and Alexis

Contents

Foreword

Few people, whatever their political views, would dispute the statement that the postwar years have seen a steady and relentless decline in Britain's relative position as a major industrial power. Indeed there are whole areas of manufacturing industry where Britain once led the world and is now no longer a major international force.

The reasons for this depressing trend are many and extremely complex. In the early 1960s Harold Wilson introduced the concept of the need to introduce the 'white heat of the technological revolution'. It was a good political slogan because it encapsulated a widespread, but over-simplified, belief that the British problem was basically the result of a failure to invest in the modernisation of capital equipment and technological innovation.

Other pundits have taken a longer-term view and argued that the educational and class systems in Britain are the cause, while others choose their particular object of blame from an almost endless list – from the tax system to the trade unions to the electoral system.

Personally I am in no doubt that at least one major ingredient of the problem has been, and in many cases still is, the inability of large areas of British management and shop-floor workers to identify and adapt to a new and more successful working environment.

The British-owned car industry is a classic example. Leaving aside overseas markets, the British domestic market has seen a strong and steady growth in car ownership over the last twenty years. Yet over the same period we have seen an equally steady decline in the truly British motor-car industry to a point where it has almost ceased to exist.

Despite this, Nissan, the world's fourth-largest car manufacturer, has committed itself to a massive investment in the UK and has already been highly successful in establishing itself with a British labour force, British managers and a British trade union. The only new element was the introduction of and, with some adaptation to accommodate a very different culture, insistence on the Nissan/Japanese management techniques and philosophy.

For decades it has been widely accepted that the management

of British industry, particularly in the field of labour relations, must take some of the blame for the relative decline in the country's economic performance. In the 1950s and 1960s comparisons were frequently made with the techniques and performance of American management. More recently, however, attention has been increasingly focused upon the obvious success of Japanese companies working in countries with very different cultures from their own.

The speed with which Japanese industry has expanded overseas has been phenomenal. The total value of Japanese direct overseas investment is around $84 billion and well over half that has taken place in the last five years.

Paradoxically the United Kingdom, despite the appalling and frequently exaggerated criticisms of its labour force, has become the first choice of Japanese companies wishing to invest in Europe. Courted by most European governments with large grants, tax concessions and almost free factory sites, Japanese investment in the United Kingdom is already double that of any other European country and growing rapidly.

Until recently however most Japanese companies in the UK were engaged in light assembly employing a high proportion of unskilled or semi-skilled workers. In addition to his considerable experience of labour relations in large British and American companies, Peter Wickens's total involvement with the establishment of a major Japanese manufacturing plant in the UK is almost, if not totally, unique.

Although Datsun cars, as they were previously known, had been available in the UK for many years, they were distributed and sold by a private company. Nissan itself did not have an office or a single employee in this country until 1983. Of course, as one of the world's largest motor-car manufacturers, Nissan has established and successfully managed many overseas subsidiaries. Despite that, as the Company's UK Adviser, I was in no doubt that the project could only succeed if the attitudes and practices of both management and shopfloor workers were markedly different from those traditional to the British motor-car industry. That this has been achieved is apparent to anyone who visits the Sunderland factory. Speak to members of the workforce and their enthusiasm and commitment to the company and the product are as obvious as they are regrettably unusual.

The author's experience of American methods, while working

with Continental Can, helped him to adapt to the much more radical differences of the Japanese approach of Nissan. The British have many qualities, but the ability to adapt easily to new ways has not historically been the most obvious of them.

In contrast one of the key elements in the economic success of Japan has been their ability to identify their weaknesses and adapt to new ways. It is a paradox that while many Westerners are having a love affair with Japanese management philosophy there is in Japan increasing interest in what are perceived to be positive features of the US management style. Job-switching, head-hunting and takeovers, even hostile ones, are beginning to creep into Japanese corporate life. Even the much-vaunted consensus style of decision-making is under fire at a time when speed of decision-making can be the key to survival.

The Japanese culture permeates every area of Japanese activity, and management techniques are very different from the traditional British approach. But they are simply different, there is nothing mysterious about them. There are lessons we can learn which would lead to an improvement in many areas of industry, and therefore our competitiveness.

Mr Ishihara, Chairman of Nissan, in an interesting comment summed up the possibilities when he said 'If Western industry succeeds in matching Japanese productivity life could be very tough indeed for Japanese industry. This is a bigger problem (for Japan) than the rise of the newly industrialised countries which are only strong in certain sectors.'

It will be sad if we fail to learn from the success of others.

RICHARD MARSH

Acknowledgements

As I am a full-time practitioner, this book has been written in those few spare hours available at weekends. As a result the disturbance to family life has been considerable. But, in addition, my wife, Helga, ended up by typing 90 per cent of the manuscript and my son, Alexis, spent large amounts of time finding out how to operate the newly-acquired word processor. To them my sincere and grateful thanks.

On a professional level I am deeply indebted to the work of three organisations: Industrial Relations Services, Incomes Data Services and the Work Research Unit of ACAS who regularly provide significant amounts of information invaluable to the practitioner who does not have the time to undertake lengthy personal visits to organisations. The chapter, 'Japanese management – separating reality from the myth' was much influenced by my experience in working with many Japanese but in particular I wish to thank Hiroshi Moriyama whose ability to analyse and clarify many initial contradictions was invaluable, not only in the writing of this book, but also on a practical basis in bringing together the Japanese and British cultures.

A constant theme of this book is that success depends on what happens at the sharp end of the business. Therefore the greatest contribution of all has been made by the people I have worked with – throughout my career – in Central Electricity Generating Board, Ford Motor Company, Continental Can Company, British Gas Corporation and Nissan. Without them, nothing could have been achieved.

PETER WICKENS

Introduction: The View from Abroad

Without doubt the greatest concern of the potential inward investor to the UK is this country's industrial relations record – or at least the stereotype as presented by the international media. Twenty years ago the one British name known to small boys and businessmen throughout the world was Bobby Charlton. Today – particularly among Asian businessmen – there are three names, Princess Diana, Margaret Thatcher and Arthur Scargill. While in the business community the first two are admired, the latter serves only to reinforce their prejudices. No amount of statistical analysis showing the considerably reduced level of strikes or the fact that in the international league table of industrial action Britain is by no means the worst can overcome this stereotype, which from time to time we inexorably seem to reinforce.

In an attempt to better educate the potential inward investor the National Economic Development Office published a booklet[1] in 1979 specifically aimed at explaining Britain's industrial relations system. Quoting a study of the incidence of stoppages[2] it concluded that 'strikes tended to occur most frequently in certain industries, for example coal-mining, port transport and motor vehicles, and generally in larger plants with, say, 1000 or more employees. Over manufacturing industry as a whole, 95 per cent of plants were stoppage-free in the three-year period of the study. As in other walks of life, it is often the failures that are reported. The thousands of differences large and small which have been settled by reasonable discussion between management and shop stewards go unreported.[1] The Japanese businessman reading this looks not at the 95 per cent which are strike-free, but asks about the five per cent, one out of twenty, which have experienced strikes and wants to know about the 'thousands of differences'. He fails to understand how you can have 'thousands of differences' – even if they are resolved!

Unfortunately there is much that is not contained in the official statistics, which are collected on a voluntary basis through Unemployment Benefit Offices, nationalised industries, large firms, newspaper reports, etc. The statistics do not include that vast majority of stoppages which last for twenty minutes, two

1

hours, half a shift etc. and which, while involving only a few people, have a disproportionate effect on the operation of the unit. They do not include the countless management hours that are spent in frustrating discussions seeking to prevent a 'difference' becoming a dispute. When the NEDO refers to 'reasonable discussions between managements and shop stewards' they clearly have not been close to a management team which has to spend a vast proportion of its time dealing with people-related problems. Neither do they take account of the many desirable changes which are simply not brought forward because of the known hassles which will occur – with no guarantee of eventual success. Or, if the change *is* introduced, the maximum potential benefits are so watered down that the effort will have hardly been worth it. The greatest cry from the heart at Ford in the troubled times of the early seventies used to come from the then Dagenham Body and Assembly General Operations Manager, Bill Collard, 'Don't they understand?' Fortunately in some areas there are now signs that 'they' (we) do.

In British industry in the 1970s (and now) the call was for predictability, i.e. that everyone would arrive for work and stay there, working, until the time to go home. To a certain extent the major set-piece stoppages over pay and conditions, while damaging, can be handled. In not knowing what will happen on a day-to-day basis, the UK, if not unique among industrialised nations, is certainly around the bottom of this league table.

While it can be argued that this is a one-sided picture and clearly there has been a dramatic improvement in recent years (1.9 million days lost in 1986 compared with a 1975 to 1984 average of 11.1 million days lost) it *is* the picture that the potential inward investor brings with him. In Japan, and to a slightly lesser extent in the United States, a full day's production means just that – people being at their place of work at the start of shift – not clocking on at that time with a subsequent catching up by working along the line or faster on a sub-assembly operation. Unfortunately this attitude is repeated throughout the day with extensions to tea breaks, lunch breaks and an early finish so that people clock out on the bell rather than finish work at that time. While it can be argued that by catching up or working ahead production is not lost this is not always true and if standard times are properly established (which, most likely, they are not) quality will suffer.

But then according to the view of the inward investor, the British worker is not particularly concerned with quality – and in this he is echoing the view of his management who reinforce this lack of interest by introducing large numbers of Inspectors. Their task is to identify faults and thus the attitude develops that 'If I don't get it right it will be picked up!' Of course, British management *does* pay attention to quality but the attitude is one of 'Give me the required schedule and make sure the quality is right' whereas in Japan it is 'Give me the quality and if you can't, don't build the schedule'. The different starting point says a lot. The amount of production management blood shed on the fields of British industry over schedules not being met compared to that over poor quality has been like the flow from a severed artery compared to the droplet from a pinprick!

If the Japanese businessman does not understand the British attitude to quality he is dumbfounded by our attitude to flexibility. Until the 1985/86 negotiations Ford, within the five-grade wage structure, had over 500 separate job titles (most of which were unused) but has now reduced these to around 50. The electricity supply industry, which was one of the first UK organisations to start down the harmonisation road, still retains some 60 job titles for its manual workers including more than 20 different types of craftsman. The essential point is not the absolute number but the fact that it is symptomatic of the worker trying to protect jobs by erecting demarcations, and management trying to rigidly define jobs for the purpose of job evaluation. Both have the effect of reducing flexibility and seem to be designed to prevent British industry adapting rapidly to the changing requirements of the market place. It is this fear of inheriting reactionary attitudes and restrictive practices that is a major factor in persuading so many inward investors to opt for greenfield sites – often away from the traditional centres of their industry.

The actual capability of British management is frequently questioned abroad. The Western propensity to go for short term returns rather than long term benefits is not understood by the Japanese in particular. But when this attitude in the UK is combined with the poor status of industry, the low level of qualifications – particularly of production management – and the apparent lack of commitment to the view that the Company comes first, the Americans and Japanese are highly sceptical of the ability of local nationals to actually run their companies should they invest in the UK. In this, of course, they are adopting nothing more than the early postwar British attitude to the then colonies – but then of course *we* were superior (!). Somehow it seems different when you are on the receiving end.

With all of these problems it is inconceivable that the *potential* investor should become an *actual* investor. However, many have. Whatever the business, the starting point is the desire to make a profit. To the Japanese the desire to manufacture within the EEC and, with an appropriate local content, to have access to European markets with relaxed market restrictions is very strong. Such was the case with Nissan. Continental Can Company, an American multinational, saw the opportunity of achieving a significant share of the British market using the new two-piece can manufacturing technology and thus gain both a technological and cost advantage over the largest British manufacturer. Empty cans are full of air and cannot be economically transported over long distances.

The basic reasons for investing overseas are many but once the corporate will is expressed all such companies undertake their research, and paramount in this is an in-depth analysis of the British industrial relations scene. The conclusion they reach (or at least those who do decide positively – we hear little of the negatives) is that the positive attributes in the UK are such that, while they may have to change much of what has gone before, change and subsequent success *are* possible.

The author has been directly involved in bringing about such change in two companies – first as Director of Human Resources with Continental Can Company (UK) Ltd. and then as Director of Personnel of Nissan Motor Manufacturing (UK) Ltd. (NMUK). In both companies we undertook an extensive study of what is happening in industry, not only in the UK but anywhere where there was something to learn. There is much that one can be optimistic about but there is no magic formula – no 'flavour of the month' panacea for all our ills. All any of us can do is what is right for our own company and that may be very different to the answer for others. However, wherever one looks, common themes do begin to emerge and a purpose of this book is to identify those themes which do seem to have a relevance beyond the specific.

The book is however, in part, also a record of the processes undertaken in setting up two companies. It is not an academic work. No special research has been undertaken and most of the sources are those available to the busy practitioner. Any omissions are therefore those of one who has limited time to undertake a real task. It may therefore be of interest to the academic to learn what really influences the practitioner and the thought processes pursued in developing policies and practices. Nor does the book include any discussion on matters with which I have not been directly involved, e.g. profit-sharing schemes, or of government legislation which, on a day-to-day basis, is not directly relevant to the practitioner.

The book is addressed to fellow practitioners, directors, managers, staff, trade unionists, academics and students in an industrial or commercial environment. No-one should waste time trying to re-invent the wheel and no-one should simply imagine that, because one particular notion or method is currently successful, that approach can be transferred to another country or company. Too many consultants make a good living out of trying to persuade us otherwise. However, as indicated, certain common themes do emerge and if the reader finds that only a small part of what follows is relevant to his or her circumstances but that part can be effectively utilised, the purpose of the book will have been achieved. The essential point is not to say 'It's all right for you, you've had a greenfield site' or as has been said to Eaton Ltd 'Your Manchester factory burned down' or to Nabisco 'You had millions of American dollars' but to think strategically and say 'This is possible – I can get there in six years time if I plan properly and take people with me'. The special circumstances of others are not an excuse for doing nothing! If at the same time we are able to make a contribution to changing the view of the potential inward investor towards what is possible in British employee relations that will be a double benefit.

However, a word of warning. Companies are not in the employee relations business, any more than they are in the cost control business, industrial engineering business etc. They are in business to sell profitably a product desired by the customer. Though employee relations might be exemplary, if the product is of poor quality, the design bad, or the market changes, the company can go out of business or the factory close. A number of companies, favourably quoted in this book, have closed their operations which, despite good employee relations, have lost their market. Good employee relations can help but cannot create a market where none exists. It is sometimes salutory to remind ourselves of this.

1 'Them and Us' ... to Just 'Us'

NOTE: Throughout this book the terms 'single status' and 'common terms and conditions of employment' are interchanged. While academic distinctions may be made between the various phrases no distinction is made in these pages. However, in my view the term 'single status' is a misnomer. It is simply not possible for everyone to have the same status in an organisation – the plant manager has a different status to the supervisor or to the line worker simply because of the positions held. Nothing will change that, for status is a state of mind – your perception of your position in relation to another. What we *can* do however is to eliminate many of the differences in the way we treat people and end up with the same or similar employment packages. Thus the term 'common terms and conditions of employment' is more accurate. It is, however, cumbersome and will not always be used.

'THEM AND US'

Many historical factors account for the differences in terms and conditions of employment of manual and non-manual workers. In the mid-nineteenth century, education for the children of the poor was almost non-existent and the manual worker was invariably illiterate, for his life style simply did not require him to read or write. On the other hand, since mediaeval times, the church and, subsequently, the business community did need to employ an educated minority. Their tasks were to copy manuscripts, undertake correspondence, keep accounts etc. and thus almost by definition there grew a close relationship, often an identity, between the master and his clerk. The clerk knew as much, if not more, about the business than the master.

With the emergence of an industrial society in the mid-19th century, the close relationship between the clerk and the master – now often an engineer – was reinforced. Charles Booth in *Life and Labour of the People in London*[1] described the master–clerk

7

relationship thus: 'The value of a clerk's services thus depends closely and somewhat curiously on relations with his employer. The achievement of high economic and social status is the result of a happy conjunction of appropriate talents with diligent, tactful and personal association with a particular employer'. The picture was not wholly rosy however. William Cobbett describing his early life as a clerk stated that the experience was 'wholly unattended by pleasure... The office (for so the dungeon where I wrote was called) was so dark that on cloudy days we were obliged to burn candles. I worked like a galley slave from five in the morning until eight or nine at night and sometimes all night long. I never quitted this gloomy recess except on Sundays.'[2]

Another contemporary view of the role of the post-industrial revolution clerk was given by C. E. Parsons in 1876. 'Clerks are as a rule of decent appearance and gentlemanly habits, patient and long suffering, not given to noisily insisting about their rights and are possessed of some delicacy when requesting an advance of salary, not unnaturally believing that their employers ought to recognise their merits and reward their careful guardianship of trade secrets and the valuable information they frequently obtain, without requiring somewhat humiiiating reminders'[3] – not like those manual workers!

Clerks included not only the sons of the wealthy but also 'meanly dressed, anxious faced, half fed mortals who dine in Wapping at the fourpence halfpenny hall...'[4] In both cases however the clerk had to know the business and it was open to him to progress to the more senior positions in the profession. Contrast this with the manual worker who was considered by the employer to be nothing more than a factor of production – a tool in the manufacturing process.

This attitude was reinforced by the twentieth-century development of scientific management, which focused all attention on the production process. The manual worker was regarded very much as economic man, responding to stimuli and being penalised for inattention, lateness etc. He was subject to being laid off at a moment's notice if no work was available and in such circumstances received no pay beyond the hour he worked. At no time was the manual worker considered to have any identity with the company. At no time was he trusted to work without supervision or control. To pay more than an hour at a time would be to accept an obligation which could lead the company to ruin! In some industries and companies such an attitude has only recently died away – in others it may possibly remain.

Thus from mediaeval times through to the present day, the white-collar class has been distinguished from the manual worker. Not only because of the work they did – for often the master in the late ninteenth century was more an engineer than an administrator and thus spent much time on practical matters – but perhaps because of the dependency of the master on the clerk. Their culture and dress were more that of the employer than the manual worker. As George Bain puts it, this distinction was emphasised by the employers who were 'prepared to honour the white-collar workers' claims. Indeed they even fostered them by encouraging white-collar workers to identify their interests with those of the employers, and to regard themselves as having a personal relationship with them'.[5]

The growth of modern industry has only served to emphasise these differences. The increasing dependence on an administrative cadre has led in many companies to the view that the indirect service areas are more important than the direct production activities – the planners are more important than the doers. One has large areas of discretion and the other small; one has high involvement and the other low; one is committed to the company, the other is not. Whether or not the manual/non-manual split could have evolved any differently is not a subject for debate in this book. However, in most companies, the 'them' and 'us' syndrome still dominates even though many managements like to delude themselves that 'in our company we're one big family'. Thus in Continental, when reviewing the options, we concluded that in much of British industry we were in a vicious downward spiral among manual workers of inflexibility, poor cooperation, low productivity chased down by, and chasing, lack of trust, low rewards, poor security and so on. But, we concluded, there were pressures for change...

... TO JUST 'US'

Although in many industries there is currently a feeling of 'Adapt or Die' the pressures for change from the 'Them and Us' syndrome have been evident for the last thirty years or more. This has been evident in both successful and unsuccessful companies and indeed it could be said that it is the successful who are most likely to adapt or, perhaps, they are successful *because* they have adapted. The argument is circular.

For the majority of the postwar period, full employment was regarded as a prime economic objective with the key to profitability being an increase in employee productivity. Success therefore has depended to a large extent on employee co-operation and goodwill. While in the 1980s full employment has not been *the* prime economic objective of the government, the constrained economic circumstances of most companies have made the need for employee co-operation and commitment paramount. This, combined with other factors such as improved education and universal communication, has led to a questioning of the traditional attitudes to work and, indeed, to all aspects of society.

In the United Kingdom the 1944 Education Act provided the postwar impetus to major changes in the UK educational system and, while there may be debate over the comparative standards of education following the introduction of the comprehensive system, there can be little doubt that since 1945 overall standards of education and information have risen. This is both cause and effect of the accelerating acceptance of the so-called new technology in modern industry.

Earlier production methods clearly defined the separate roles of those who laboured in, supervised and administered the manufacturing process. Modern technology is blurring many of these distinctions. In the continuous process industries the work of monitoring machinery and equipment often requires a higher level of knowledge and responsibility for the efficient use of expensive machinery than was ever the case previously, but at the same time the routine exercise of craft skills in such work has diminished. On the other hand sophisticated methods of quality control, maintenance and trouble-shooting on advanced electronic equipment has resulted in the inspector and electrician becoming technologists rather than craftsmen. The need for increased productivity as well as the requirements of the equipment has led to demands for increasing flexibility and a consequential increase in multi-skills which, though to many it remains a pipe dream, is being achieved in a growing number of companies (see Chapter 3).

Many traditional white-collar jobs using pen and paper have changed beyond all recognition – even the early jobs of the computer revolution are now disappearing with the almost universal application of VDU's. The amount of information available to the British Gas Customer Service Clerk today would have required an army of Senior Clerks a few short years ago. But now, with the movement of computers to the shop floor, many so-called manual workers are using these machines for what they really are – highly efficient tools. Following the initial antagonistic reaction of the trade union movement to the introduction of new technology it is instructive to read the 1979 TUC booklet *Employment and Technology*[6] which stated 'Technological change and the micro electronics revolution are a challenge but also an opportunity. There is the challenge that the rapid introduction of new processes and work organisation will lead to the loss of many jobs and growing social dislocation. Equally however there is the realisation that new technologies also offer great opportunities – not just for increasing the competitiveness of British industry but for increasing the quality of working life and for providing new benefits to working people'.

This constructive approach was reflected in the negotiating strategy which recommended that negotiators seek a guarantee of 'No redundancy' but accepted that job changes within the organisation could be necessary. While approved by the Congress this document never really got off the ground because the CBI, after initially indicating that it found favour, withdrew, probably when it discovered that companies were gaining acceptance without a CBI–TUC understanding. Today, in many companies the acceptance of new technology on the shop floor is a fact of life. People have come to terms with it, welcome its introduction and, once familiar with its capabilities, frequently seek new ways of using this new tool.

As the tools of the trade are changing so are the responsibilities. Again within British Gas it is really inconceivable that the Service Engineer (although really a fitter – not a professional engineer), who is the prime contact with the customer and whose responsibilities are no less than the clerk's back at the office, should be treated differently to that clerk. In many fields the manual worker has greater responsibilities than the administrator.

In the early 1970s the main political parties all made clear statements on the elimination or reduction of status differentials. The Code of Practice which followed the Conservative gov-

ernment's 1971 Industrial Relations Act stated 'Differences in the
conditions of employment and status of different categories of
employee and the facilities available to them should be based on
the requirements of the job. The aim should be progressively to
remove differences which are not so based. Management employees and their representatives should cooperate in working
towards this objective'.[7]

The previous Labour Government's White Paper *In Place of
Strife*[8] urged employers 'to examine fully and sympathetically the
possibility of removing unnecessary and outdated distinctions
between 'staff' and 'other employees'. The Liberals 'Employees
Charter Bill' of 1973 dealt with almost every aspect of employees'
rights and proposed that unnecessary distinctions between
employees should be eliminated within a given four-year period.

All these factors have clearly influenced British management
which corporately and individually is increasingly questioning
the ethics of distinguishing between different categories of
employee, particularly when the demands made on the manual
worker exceed those of the administrator, and the flexibility and
co-operation of the skilled craftsman is more important for the
success of the enterprise than the attitude of the typist, clerk or
draughtsman. Some Trade Unions were not slow to express their
views over these developments. In 1975 a conference of the,
then, General and Municipal Workers Union passed the following resolution: 'Congress urges the establishment of one-status
companies. It is farcical where for example a junior office girl
joins a company and is immediately eligible for far greater
benefits than an employee with possibly 20 or 30 years service'.
Even earlier, Jim Conway, in 1965 the General Secretary of the
Amalgamated Engineering Union, when writing in the Union's
Journal[9] said that the aims of staff grade agreements (defined by
him as the elimination of unnecessary overtime without loss of
output or earnings and the narrowing and eventual abolition of
the gap between staff and manual workers) were consistent with
the aims of TU policy.

Murlis and Grist interviewed a number of union officials for
their BIM study *Towards Single Status*[10] and found that they
believed 'single-status agreements will come in time as joint
negotiations by manual and non-manual unions improve and as
companies change their attitude towards the relative value of
different categories of employee'. The manual union representa-

tives were however doubtful about the success of the idea and one was quoted as saying 'This Union has always pursued a policy of negotiations for improvements in benefits on a one by one basis rather than negotiating for staff status. The concept of single status had a great deal of appeal ... but it was found that once negotiations started it was impossible not to go back to the piecemeal situation. This does not however preclude matching up with an employer's rolling programme'.

The early attitude of some trade unions towards harmonisation may be summarised by their evidence to the Court of Enquiry into the electricity supply dispute over their staff status agreement in 1964. 'We are not so much interested in achieving status as we are in achieving the benefits of status enjoyed by staff workers in the matter of wages, hours and fringe benefits. In seeking to achieve these benefits we seek to eliminate status distinction in industry. We are not interested over-much in acquiring for manual workers the status symbols of the white-collar workers.' This contrasts with the experience of Shell at Teesport where in a greenfields situation they sought the early involvement of the TGWU. In a heavily industrialised area with numerous local and national agreements the Company stated that it wanted to negotiate a separate and completely different type of agreement. After seeking the agreement of their national officials the local TU officers entered fully into the discussions, proved receptive to Shell's ideas and fully contributed in joint discussions to their development. In the second half of the 1980s many trade union claims, particularly in the automotive manufacturing industry (and, perhaps, influenced by Nissan) have laid great emphasis on harmonisation. Managements, having been responsible for developing the concept, are now often in a situation where they are having to react rather than initiate – and, as in the case of Austin Rover, the unions are surprised at management positive response.

When a change is proposed in an already existing multi-union situation the attitude of the traditional white-collar union may not always be encouraging. There remains a great deal of pride in retaining the previous differentials or, if they are not to be maintained, at least they should be equalised upwards with both staff and manual workers going for the better of the two packages. Very much aware of this possibility the Engineering Employers' Federation in its July 1980 Statement on

Harmonisation[11] said it 'undertakes continually to review differences in conditions of employment between manual and staff employees and wherever appropriate to consider courses of action which will encourage the gradual removal of all unjustified differences'. Nevertheless in relation to holidays it urged 'Where staff holiday entitlement is already in excess of the new manual workers' holiday entitlement no improvements should be made to the staff holiday entitlement. The differential should be allowed to reduce, with the aim of eventual harmonisation of the holiday entitlement at five weeks annual holiday'.

In 1979, when undertaking the initial discussion with trade unions for Continental, none of the Regional and National Officials of the TGWU, GMB, AEU, National Graphical Association, EETPU and Iron and Steel Trades Confederation expressed any significant resistance to the concept of common terms and conditions of employment – provided the terms and conditions were right – and all considered that their union was capable of representing everybody covered by such an agreement. Similarly in 1984 when preparing the contract for Nissan not one trade union official of the TGWU, GMB or AEU indicated any opposition to the concept. Particularly in a greenfields site there was a clear acceptance that common terms and conditions was 'an idea whose time had come'.

Within this overall framework the pressure for change is evident on both sides of the Atlantic. In the United States, individual companies have determined their own reasons. The Polaroid Corporation in Massachusetts is quoted in the *Harvard Business Review*[12] as basing their unification programme on the premise that 'adults should be treated as adults'. The Kinetic Dispersion Corporation of New York (manufacturers of equipment for the food and paint industry) were influenced by their President's view that he could find no justification for a two-tiered wage system. When researching for the proposals to present to the US management of Continental it was helpful to find examples of American companies that had taken this route, and in the UK the three most celebrated were all in the field of high technology, Texas Instruments, IBM and Hewlett Packard. All three have always adopted a management philosophy that all employees should have similar terms, conditions and fringe benefits. IBM in particular has clearly defined what it means by single status. Howard Gibson, then Manager, Personnel Relations of IBM United Kingdom Ltd. expressed in an article in *Industrial Participation*[13] the eight tenets of IBM's single-status philosophy: full employment, fairness in promotion, pay for performance, equal opportunity, common terms and conditions of employment, no artificial barriers, open communications channels and appeals procedure. Single-status to IBM clearly goes further than the limited definition of common terms and conditions which many companies prefer to use. This does not mean that the other companies do not adopt the other facets of the IBM philosophy but IBM's approach in pulling all these factors together remains something special.

Another US-owned company, G. D. Searle, working in the pharmaceutical industry in Northumberland stated 'We had a new factory, almost a new workforce and we wanted to get rid of the less logical differences'. Sony Corporation, manufacturers of TV sets in South Wales, stated that the elimination of illogical differences and the attempt to get their employees to identify with the aims of the company were their prime reasons. Shell Oil when developing its refinery in Teesport in 1968 considered that 'Teesport clearly offered a great opportunity not only to put into practice the ideas of the philosophy statement concerning job design but also to establish a set of working conditions and practices which could serve as a model for the older refineries to try to follow'.

Since the time of the Continental decision to establish common terms and conditions many other companies have made the decision to go down this route. Inmos regarded single-status as essential for creating a sense of common purpose among its workforce. Toshiba, when taking over the manufacturing facilities of the previous Rank Toshiba plant in Plymouth, was looking for a completely new start and approach and in particular was seeking complete flexibility of operations. Whitbread in its Magor brewery wanted to create a workforce with totally flexible attitudes and considered that single status would assist this. Carerras-Rotham in its new plant in Spennymore, Co. Durham, wanted labour flexibility and employees to have a high level of commitment. In established Companies such as Berger Paints, Plessey Controls, Rolls-Royce and Letraset, a more gradual approach resulted in progress to harmonisation accompanied by more flexible working practices and the greater acceptance of new technology. Other earlier examples of harmonisation included the electricity supply industry and ICI and both announced specific objectives – the electricity supply industry being concerned to achieve flexible working patterns and ICI to improve efficiency. The ICI explanatory booklet issued to employees in 1965 said 'It is in the interests of both the Company and its employees to achieve and maintain the highest level of efficiency in all the Company's activities and to see that the ICI payment structure and conditions of employment are designed to fit in with the industrial world into which we are rapidly moving'.

The BIM survey[14] suggested eleven reasons for companies harmonising their agreements.

Social/political climate	To increase employee cooperation
Union pressure	To improve relations with unions
Effect of legislation	To increase productivity
Shortage of unskilled Labour	To reduce labour turnover
Foreign influence	To reduce absenteeism
	To keep down wage bills

Although not originally presented in this way, the reasons listed on the left are clearly reactions to external influences but those on the right are described in terms of internal objectives – benefits to be gained. Of the stated objectives the factor most frequently cited for reducing differentials was 'To increase employee cooperation'.

Perhaps the most clearly defined policy statement is quoted in the BIM survey.[15] An unnamed profitable large holding company stated that 'Single-status is a desirable innovation because:

1. It is morally right.
2. It can help change attitudes and make a contribution to providing a more equitable industrial relations climate.
3. It is a necessary step towards a long term aim of co-determination and co-responsibility.
4. In times of full employment it aids recruitment and helps retain labour.
5. It can help achieve flexibility among the work force.'

Most of the mature companies that have adopted the policy of single status are unable to go 'all the way' at one time. As the process is almost inevitably one of levelling up it can be costly, but just as important are the difficulties associated with bringing together many disparate groups to achieve a commonality. One of the most ambitious exercises in this arena was at the Rogerstone plant of Alcan Sheet Limited which in a multi-union situation (seven trade union groups) found that over the years it had established four holiday plans, five job evaluation systems, seven wage and salary structures, three working weeks and six overtime arrangements. By involving academics and consultants as external catalysts, Alcan succeeded in bringing all their unions together and developed what they called a Single Integrated Reward Structure (SIRS) which had the aim of paying all employees on a continuous grade structure with all employees on an annual salary (although existing weekly paid had the choice of so remaining).

SIRS however had many more aims, and one cornerstone was that secondary conditions for employment should be harmonised and in the words of the 'Pay structure special' information sheet distributed in May 1979. 'It is the area where we have had the greatest difficulty in reaching agreements. Some people still question the necessity of it and undoubtedly some see the provisions as a worsening of their conditions. It has been our aim to provide a package of conditions that is understood by all, is seen as fair and does not create social or status differences'. The search for a solution to the Alcan problem began in the 1970s and it was not until June 1979 that SIRS was fully implemented. It included one site agreement, a joint council, a common salary scale, annual salary for all, no overtime, one sick pay scheme, and a productivity scheme.

The evidence of the effects of harmonisation on the previously privileged group generally shows that while there may be some initial resentment, the basic logic of eliminating the status differentials was understood. The BIM survey showed non-manual resentment to be a problem in less than 10 per cent of companies. The *Harvard Business Review* survey of the five US companies[16] concluded that many supervisors resisted the initial implementation of these programmes, partly out of confusion and partly out of fear of added responsibility. However over a period of time and with proper guidelines and support from management these fears abated and supervisors took the administrative and judgemental responsibilities in their stride.

Those UK-based companies which introduced comprehensive single-status schemes on greenfield sites have reported few conceptual difficulties among their supervisors, although this was of course partly due to the fact that in their selection process, they were careful only to appoint those people they believed would have no difficulty in adapting to a single-status structure. Learning from this lesson, the selection procedures, both in Continental and Nissan, emphasised the attitudinal aspects which were as important as the technical capability of the candidates and, as shown in Chapter 10, the Nissan selection process in particular was comprehensively designed to bring out this aspect.

There is no doubt that the process of harmonisation is regarded as being expensive by those companies contemplating this route. About one third of the companies in the BIM survey who had reduced differentials in holiday entitlement, pension, sick pay and hours of work, regarded increased costs as a 'problem'. What was not clear however was what was meant by a 'problem' in this context, whether the improvements were substituted for wage increases and whether the benefits equalled the costs, or, if they did, whether those benefits could have been achieved in another way. No company has published a cost benefit analysis of harmonisation, and with the vast number of variables and intangibles it is difficult to gain an accurate measure. In these circumstances the 'gut feel' of those directly involved is as accurate as any other measure (making allowances for the fact that such proponents will invariably wish to point to success). Universally the view among those companies that have fully implemented common terms and conditions of employment is that it is the only way to run a business. In 1979 Continental concluded that in ten years' time we would reflect why it took so long. While, now, the time span of that view seems a little too short, the process is well established, the conclusion inevitable and the rate of change accelerating.

Nevertheless in 1979, while few UK companies had taken common terms and conditions to their logical conclusion, Continental concluded that this was the right way. We established a number of Human Resources objectives including 'To establish an integrated compensation and benefits package which is designed to properly reward and motivate all company employees' and 'To establish policies and procedures ... which assist in achieving employee identification with the Company's aims and objectives'. To attract high quality people we needed to develop a reputation as a good employer, one which trusted its employees, which made demands on them and expected a positive response. One aspect of that reputation is the employment package, and we concluded that common terms and conditions would be one symbol of that approach. While part of a growing trend, we had the opportunity, in a greenfield site, of leapfrogging our competitors. The majority of characteristics, identified in companies having gone down this route, were apparent in Continental and thus we made the decision to take this way forward.

However, we were very much aware of a cautionary point. *Common terms and conditions of employment are no guarantee of success in achieving Company objectives.* As important is the attitude of management towards *all* aspects of employment and relationships within the plant. Poor management will fail, whatever framework is established and a good management can make a silk purse out of a sow's ear. A limited objective was therefore to make it easier for the good managers to succeed and more difficult for the bad managers to fail.

It is of critical importance that this lesson be taken on board by anyone contemplating harmonisation, single status, etc. One of the first companies in the UK to make any moves down this road was Smith, Kline and French and in preparing the ground they studied American experience. In a paper to the Industrial Society in 1967, P. Burger drew lessons from his company's survey. Primarily

Loyalty, co-operation, productivity cannot be bought by good staff conditions for manual workers or by any other means. There are enough companies who have become unionised since introducing such terms to prove this point... If attitudes are wrong, staff conditions will be seen as impositions from above or benefits secured purely by bargaining strength and can easily lead to indifference, resentment and even increased bargaining... the quality of management is just as important as the policies they apply, after all managers both make policies and apply them – or fail to do either ... staff status is no wonder drug. At best it corrects a gross anomaly in employment conditions and by removing the source of potentially considerable friction creates the conditions for constructive work relationships.

This is as true today as it was in 1967.

It is easy to get all the costs of harmonisation and none of the potential benefits – and the costs are the easy part to measure. The goal is a changed attitude but single status, while often a necessary condition, is not sufficient. Much else has to change before we genuinely change 'Them and Us' to 'Us' – and maybe it is never totally attainable. But if we do not try we certainly will not succeed. One company which is now trying is Austin Rover. In the Company's response to the 1986 pay claim a surprise element was a clear commitment to harmonisation of terms and conditions of employment, including moves towards an integrated grading structure and a single bargaining unit. A formidable task in such an organisation but an imaginative step which presents a challenge to both the manual and staff unions.

This new initiative was perhaps influenced by the Nissan agreement, for in the years between preparing the ground for Continental's approach and beginning a similar process with Nissan, the climate changed considerably in the UK. With Nissan there was no need to go through the lengthy process of accumulating the evidence necessary to gain acceptance of the principle of single status. Indeed at the foundation stone ceremony of the Nissan plant, held in November 1984, the Chairman of the Company, Mr Takashi Ishihara, stated 'We have four major pillars in our management philosophy for the car plant. First to have open and frank communications within the Company. Second to realise single status for all employees. Third to provide equal opportunity of promotion for every employee. And last to have complete flexibility in production operations.' To Nissan, single status was a fact of life.

On a practical basis, the Japanese simply could not understand why in ninety per cent of engineering companies the typical manual worker was on a 39 hour week and the typical 'staff' worker on 37½ hours. The staff worker had longer holidays, better sickness benefit and pension schemes – the list is almost endless. There really can be no justification for white-collar workers having better conditions than blue-collar. Indeed it could with some logic be argued that the differentials should be reversed. Thus, in Nissan we determined from the outset that we would opt for common terms and conditions of employment.

But with the earlier words of warning in mind we determined that common terms and conditions had to form but one part of a totally integrated philosophy. This was the objective in both Continental and Nissan. It meant examining the whole management style – the framework within which common terms were to be introduced as well as the common terms themselves. For Nissan, to achieve this management style meant not only looking at what was happening elsewhere in Britain, but also a study of what we could learn from the Japanese. First we had to separate the reality from the myth.

2 Japanese Management – Separating Reality from the Myth

Seven quotations:

'Local employees, unlike Japan employees, do not consider their work to be the centre of their lives. If push comes to shove, they consider work something they have to do to live.'

'Reasons for the difficulty in ordering overtime were given by 14 out of 32 responding companies as "the employees giving too much emphasis to their private lives".'

'40 per cent of 92 responding companies indicated they experienced cases where overtime was necessary but the employees refused to obey orders.'

'West European employees ... differ considerably in mentality from their Japanese counterparts.'

'Labour-management relations in Europe differ from the conciliatory type relations in Japan and derive from the class system.'

'In Japan, there is a tendency to regard paid holidays as a privilege, where workers in the West take their vacation as a right. The difference here is one of national character.'

'The rate of absenteeism is lower in Japan than it is in the West. This seems to arise from differences in work ethics directly and indirectly based on religious values.'

All of these quotations come from the Japanese themselves. In September 1985 the Japan External Trade Organisation (JETRO) published a study *State of Operations of Japanese Affiliates (Manufacturing) in Europe*.[1] Based on a questionnaire completed by 119 Japanese companies operating in Europe the survey aimed to 'obtain a grasp of the state of operations of Japanese affiliates in Europe'. However, as the first five quotations show, the commentary also gives an interesting impression of the Japanese view of certain cultural and attitudinal differences. The final two quotations relating to attitudes on vacation and absenteeism are from Nissan's own publication *Things you want to know about Nissan and Japan*[2]

The Nissan publication also states 'The salient characteristics of Japanese-style management are the lifetime employment system, the seniority system for salaries and promotions, company unions, company welfare, in-house employee education and conference-oriented integrated management.' These characteristics are however the manifestations of something much deeper which permeates every aspect of Japanese business and social life. Again, rather than quoting Western sources it is interesting to see how the Japanese themselves perceive this. Quoting the Nissan publication:

> The Japanese people tend to value group harmony more than individuality. Given the presence of this deep-rooted element in Japanese culture it is not surprising that group-oriented ideas have been adopted in corporate management practices.

> ... there is a belief in Japan that a person who works diligently will gain social recognition and work is regarded as something of a virtue.... In Japan moreover it is felt that work is an integral part of a person's life, and consequently that it should be enjoyable; this leads to independent efforts on the part of workers to improve their jobs and to upgrade the quality of their work. In addition since changing jobs is relatively rare in Japan the work that an individual does within the framework of a single company takes on a great deal of importance in his personal life. Therefore, there is a strong feeling that if one contributes to his company by working hard, his efforts will be rewarded and his private life will be enriched accordingly.

The picture presented by these quotations very much confirms the stereotyped view of Japanese management philosophy and represented the starting point from which NMUK attempted to assess what is and is not transferable from Japan to a European environment. However, the deeper we became involved in looking at Japanese practices the more we became convinced that the stereotype view is just that, a stereotype, and is as true, or untrue, as the stereotype of British industrial behaviour. Within Japan there are as many varieties of industrial behaviour as there are in the UK and we should talk about trends rather than absolutes. And in Japan, as in the UK, there are pressures for change, particularly to the seniority system. However, the interdependence of the various strands of the cultural system is so great, that to modify one element without having significant undesirable effects on other elements, will be extremely difficult.

Many views exist as to why the Japanese behave as they do. They are great self-analysts and their bookshops are full of academic volumes attempting to explain the cultural, ethical or logical basis of their management philosophy. Four contrasting views are given in books available in the UK. Michio Morishima[3] goes back 2500 years and traces the influence of Confucian ethics from that time to the present day. Marvin Wolf's anti-Japanese polemic *The Japanese Conspiracy*[4] is concerned with his thesis that there is a government-inspired plan to achieve economic domination of the world and includes chapters such as 'The exploited Japanese worker'. William Ouchi's *Theory Z*[5] concentrates on what actually happens in Japanese business today and attempts to determine those elements which are transferable to the West. Dick Wilson's *The Sun at Noon*[6] gives a down-to-earth assessment of the whole of modern Japan and is a good starting point for the newcomer. A reading of these four books will give an overall balanced picture of Japanese management.

Some analysts consider that there has been too much emphasis on history. Keith Thurley, one of Britain's leading 'Japanologists', has written 'Popular discussion is long on culture and short on political analysis'. He does not believe that lifetime employment, the seniority system and enterprise unions are the most important innovations. 'Far more remarkable is the combination in recent years of a thoroughgoing egalitarian emphasis on technical ability and of the systematic appraisal and utilisation of human talent. Much of this remains highly authoritarian in nature and the constant appraisal of motivation and loyalty clearly exerts great pressure on individual employees and managers. The positive element is the systematic rational use of talent and ability and constant attempts to motivate groups and project teams to solve new technical problems.'[7]

It is not the purpose of this chapter to attempt an analysis as to why the Japanese behave as they do. The Japanese ethical system built on the teaching of Confucius clearly has an influence, but so too does the fact that historically it has been a nation of mutually dependent farmers. The long period of isolation during which developed the practice of allegiance of the servant to the master and the master to the servant, no doubt played a part. The code of the warrior, *bushido*, emphasised winning but also emphasised honour in personal relationships. The first true constitution of Japan, promulgated by Prince Shotuko Taishi in AD 604 stipulated that the principle of all societies and communities was *wa* – harmony. The desire to emulate Western standards without losing Japanese values was the guiding spirit of the Meiji Restoration in 1867, which began the emergence of the nation from isolation. No doubt the fact that Japan is one of the most homogenous nations in the world – few immigrants and little inter-marriage – helps achieve an intuitional understanding within a unified culture. Losing a war and then being rebuilt by the United States with a constitution that prohibited vast spending on defence but was then used as an American provider and home base during the Korean War gave a boost to Japanese industry. The interlocking structure of the business community with its emphasis on the long-term viability of companies, which are seen as a collection of people rather than as a mechanism for a quick profit, is an important factor. Government direction of business and the targeting of market sectors with internal protection and external subsidies is relevant. The availability of cheap capital, partly due to the large supply of money resulting from high levels of personal saving ... the theories are endless.

But we are concerned with none of these theories. What matters is not the reasons – although no real understanding can be achieved without an attempt to appreciate the history and culture – but what is actually happening now. And, most importantly, what can we learn from the Japanese? While we in the West may wish to work towards many of the same objectives as the Japanese, the way in which those objectives are expressed and the manner in which we achieve them may be very different. What we have to do is to define as accurately as possible those elements of Japanese *working practices* which can be transferred and often we find that those transferable elements are not peculiar to the Japanese but are universal. The task is not to introduce *Japanese* management practices but *good* management practices. To learn what is good *and* transferable from Japan, we have to try to separate the reality from the myth.

One of the most common concepts of Japanese employment

practices is 'life-time employment' – a device originated by late 19th-century cotton spinners to restrict labour mobility. This does in fact exist – for adult males working full time for the large industrial and commercial organisations which employ around one-third of the working population. The other two thirds work variously in the service sector, often self-employed, or in the many thousands of sub contractors, who produce parts for the large conglomerates. For them, and for women, who normally work in low level jobs until they leave the workforce on marriage, lifetime employment is rarer. Even in the large corporations 'lifetime' is an exaggeration for, apart from senior executives, who may remain in post until their late sixties or seventies, most retire in their mid-fifties and then often start work in another organisation in a lower capacity to enable them to make ends meet. Others in a sufficiently senior position may transfer to a subsidiary and thus block the promotion chances of the mid-career executive not fortunate enough to join a 'blue chip' company after graduation. Even adult males in the blue chip companies have life-time employment only if they are full time workers – seasonal and temporary staff have no such benefit.

In two respects this position is changing. It is now a government requirement that organisations employing over 100 are obliged to give six per cent of their jobs to older workers. For the first time in 1984, the very large companies exceeded this figure, and a Ministry of Labour survey found that in 1985, 7.5 per cent of full-time employees in Japanese companies, with more than 100 workers, were aged over 55. For women, the 1986 Equal Employment Opportunities Law may bring about a change, but so long as women, their husbands, and very importantly, the parents, see the woman's place as being in the home, attitudes will change even more slowly than in the West. A 1985 survey of 1500 businesses reported in the Japanese newspaper *Yomiuri Shimbun*,[8] said that 53 per cent of companies offered higher starting salaries for males and 40 per cent indicated that equal promotion and salary increase systems would create problems, with early leaving being a significant factor blocking womens' progression and involvement. In any case 'an overwhelming majority' of 500 female office workers 'preferred marriage and motherhood to job responsibility.' As many as 86.6 per cent said that they had no 'interest' in or were 'not sure' if they wanted to assume managerial jobs.

But, within the more narrow confines of the definition than is usual, lifetime employment does exist. This means that once he has joined a large corporation (and this is one reason why competition to join such organisations is great) the employee can expect to remain with that company until he retires. This works two ways – the company does not expect to lay him off if the economy declines or the market changes (and to the responsible manager it would be personal disaster if he had to lay off his staff) and the employee does not expect to resign to join another organisation – indeed, if he were to, then normally he would be regarded with suspicion by his new employer, as the fact that he had not displayed commitment and loyalty to his first company could mean that the same poor attitude could be repeated. This closed labour market system remains an integral part of Japanese business practices and forms part of the interdependent seniority, lifetime employment and commitment philosophies. If you cannot move to another company you *have* to be loyal to the one you first joined. It means however that the employee can expect to be moved within his company or to a subsidiary and that such moves are necessary to meet a changing economic or market situation. It may even mean that employees can be loaned from one company to another. For example, in 1983, Nippon Steel loaned some 250 workers to Nissan to work on various assembly lines. While with the changing value of its currency Japan is having to face the prospect of rising unemployment for the first time in its recent history the blue chip companies by early 1987 remained fairly insulated from the trend – the effects mainly falling on the sub contractors. This feeling of loyalty to the Company is assisted by the fact that Japanese companies hire their graduates only once a year – in April. Students have only one chance in their life of joining a blue chip company and such companies hire frequently from the most prestigious universities – starting with the University of Tokyo. Hence there is tremendous competition to gain admission to those universities from which the blue chip companies recruit, although it is an exaggeration to say that they recruit *only* from the best universities. In this, Japanese companies are not unlike their Western counterparts. Many prestigious companies maintain links with prestigious universities and the universities with prestigious schools. There remains however, considerable parental pressure on children to do well in their education and such pressure has

resulted in the growth of the *juku* – supplementary private
education out of school hours – designed to give children the skills
necessary to pass examinations. When this is combined with a
university system which has as its prime motive the preparation of
people for engineering and business, the commitment of those who
make it through the system can almost be physically felt. Not to
succeed can mean working for a company a stage or two away from
the 'blue chip' without the trappings associated with such prestige
employment and at age 50 finding that a 'blue chip' retiree moves
into your company to a position to which you have aspired!

Peer *
Gp

    The single start date also means that you have a peer group
with whom you can identify all your working life and this, when
combined with the seniority system, gives a further impetus to
the development of loyalty. In simple terms seniority means that
salary increases and promotion are dependent upon length of
service. A 'class', who joined at the same time, will receive the
same salary increases and promotions until the first 'cut' comes.

    It is the seniority system that is seen by many Japanese as being
the aspect that is most in need of change and, indeed, it *is* changing.
Twenty years ago some 90 per cent of university graduates were
promoted to Manager after the required 15 years service. Today
the figure is 20 to 30 per cent. The traditional system, whereby
length of service determined progression and salary, has resulted
in a considerable bunching of executives at the higher levels,
people of less ability being promoted at the same rate as those of
high ability and a salary spread which is the exact opposite of that
in a Western company, i.e., taking a group with, say, twenty
years service, a Western company will have a large number at
lower salary levels and a few at higher while the situation in a
Japanese company will be the reverse. The normal progression in
a Japanese company after 15 years was to Manager and then
successively to Deputy General Manager, General Manager and
various levels of Director. With the number of Director positions
being finite but those below being less so, an arrangement
developed whereby people were allowed to progress to the title
of General Manager – and receive the pay and perks of such
position but without in fact doing the work of a General
Manager. With the number of real General Manager posts now
becoming limited, all know that some people are not doing the
real job, but they are treated as though they were. Some of these
will be the people who go to the subsidiary companies, but for

the company the cost is high and in the second half of the 1980s
cannot be sustained as it once was.

Within the Japanese system the traditional way does have its
advantages. It means for example that because someone of, say,
35 knows that he will always be senior to someone five years
younger he is not always looking over his shoulder at the 'Young
Turk' coming through to rise above him in the organisation.
Thus, because the senior man is not worried about being
overtaken in the hierarchy, he can have a genuine interest in
ensuring that the younger man is fully and properly trained.
When this is combined with the fact that both can expect to be
with the company until retirement, and the aim of harmony
within the group, the corporate interest is invariably put before
the individual.

If you ask a Japanese what he does for a living, he will tell you
that he works for Nissan, Hitachi, Sanyo, etc. If you ask a
Westerner, he will tell you that he is an electrical engineer,
personnel manager, production worker, etc. The Japanese
allegiance is to the company, the Western allegiance is to the
occupation (although in neither case is the commitment to the
exclusion of the other). The Japanese administrator, who joins
from university, will frequently not know into which department
he will be placed and will during his career expect to move from
one function to another. The engineer is less mobile but with the
Japanese emphasis on the closeness of engineering and production (which are often indistinguishable) he too will have a
broader career than his Western counterpart. As stated in the
Nissan book 'The system of lifetime employment gives employees a sense of security and a feeling of belonging. At the
same time it sustains the unique corporate style of each
enterprise; it motivates a feeling of unity among the employees
and a consciousness of sharing the same fate as the company.
Thus it can be said that lifetime employment contributes to the
group orientation that the Japanese people have towards getting
things done.'

Because of lifetime employment, Japanese companies are able
to pay particular attention to the in-house training and development of their staff. Knowing that people are going to be with you
for more than thirty years gives the company the confidence to
train and develop its staff without the fear that they will depart to
another organisation. Training does not have to be rushed;

experience can be broad and western-style specialisation is rarely allowed to develop. Indispensable 'experts' are not created and knowledge is spread around and – most importantly – is shared. The more experienced employees cooperate in improving the abilities of their younger colleagues and in this way there develops the mutual understanding of the corporate values. Japanese staff gradually acquire empathy with the values of their company and an implicit understanding of its objectives – the direction in which it is going rather than specific objectives in the western sense. This empathy underlies much of the subsequent decision-making process, which can only be successful when everyone is working in the same direction and shares the same values.

Within the Japanese culture there is a greater natural respect for authority than in the West. The stereotype of Japanese business behaviour in this area is perhaps conditioned by the respect given to age and seniority in the family. In business, however, true respect will not be accorded to the person who lacks ability although in Japan such an individual in a senior position is much more likely to be *treated* with respect than in the West. In western business we may say that respect has to be earned, particularly by the new, young man appointed to a senior position. Because 'new' and 'young' rarely occur in a Japanese senior position the need to *earn* respect is virtually unknown. In a closed labour market situation, particularly when associated with internal mobility, the 'need to get to know a person' hardly exists. Conversely, a Japanese will feel uncomfortable if he is promoted more rapidly than his peer group, particularly if this means being in charge of older people. This results, not infrequently, in individuals turning down the opportunity of early promotion.

Complementary to this, the Japanese, rather than being class-conscious in the western sense, are status-conscious. Dependent very much on the level of education and subsequently seniority in the organisation, this manifests itself in many ways. The depth of a bow will depend on a person's position in the hierarchy – the more senior, the shallower the bow in relation to the subordinate. The position of the desk is important, as is the size. In a factory, while everyone will wear the same basic workwear, the individual's rank will often be indicated by the number and width of bands around his cap – none for the production worker, one for the foreman, two for the general foreman and so on. Japanese managers often have reserved car parking spaces close to the factory while workers will have a much longer walk. Separate dining facilities for managers are justified on the same basis as in the West – 'It's the only chance we have of meeting together to talk business'. This is as little justified in Japan as it is in Britain. The job title rather than the person's name will frequently be used – and when the name is used it is always the surname rather than the first name, which is only permitted within the family. Frequently in Japan, the main entrance of a building is reserved for senior executives only. Lower level people – including managers – have to go around the side.

A company executive will have different ways of addressing his equals and subordinates, and the positions in which people sit at a meeting will be dictated by their relative seniority. While this may well happen in meetings in the West the degree of importance is very much greater in Japan. The practice of exchanging business cards is not only an extremely useful aid to remembering the names of the people to whom you will be talking but also serves to allow those meeting for the first time to accurately assess their respective positions in the hierarchy and from this their approach to each other will be determined.

It is within this system of harmony, shared values and respect for authority that the process known as consensus operates. For the westerner, consensus is perhaps one of the most difficult of the Japanese concepts to grasp, particularly as it is often presented as something peculiar to the Japanese. Thus we look for something special. In fact we should really be looking at matters of degree rather than an absolute difference, for in Japan as in the West, there is a spectrum of consensus. Japanese consensus can operate on a formal and informal basis. If there is a major decision to be made affecting many people, an individual or small group will have the task of ensuring that everyone who could possibly have an input into that decision, and whose support is necessary to make it succeed, is consulted. A paper will be prepared and views will be sought. If there is a significant modification the group will go back to those who were consulted before the change – and so on until everyone is in agreement. Each person then fixes his seal to the proposal, the *ringi* system, and is then totally committed to its implementation and success.

This process, often used to obtain formal approval of a project, is not dissimilar to a Western company's project approval system, whereby a plan to spend a significant amount of money is taken around various departments and signatures obtained before going to the final authority for sign off. Just as in the West, various levels will require change and an allowance will be built in so that the final authority can require a cost reduction to be made. Where there is a significant difference, however, is the depth of detail into which the Japanese will delve when preparing even the simplest of proposals. Many hours will be spent in the most comprehensive analysis of every alternative and while this may considerably lengthen the decision-making process, it does mean that the pre-decision analysis is far more thorough than in the West.

While on the formal basis the Japanese system is not significantly different, it is perhaps the spirit within which such consensus takes place that is special. One feels that in a Western company each individual or department would be quite happy if it did not have to bother with the others, whereas in Japan the commitment is much greater. This is evident in minor matters where such a process as *ringi* or project approval does not *need* to operate in the western sense. In the Japanese firm consensus, even on small matters, does *need* to operate. Much of this discussion is designed to eliminate potential problems. It goes into minute detail, takes considerable time and often involves larger numbers of people than would be the case in the West. As a result it takes much longer to reach a decision. When that decision is reached, however, there is a much greater degree of commitment, or, perhaps more accurately, acquiescence, and implementation is rapid. However, if problems occur, there is a much greater reluctance in Japan to change the decision – a much greater effort is made to make the new situation fit the original plan. While a totally different situation will result in a change to the Japanese plan, the tendency is to criticize if the plan needs changing whereas the westerner will be criticized if he fails to recognise that the plan needs changing. This again is a matter of degree rather than an absolute difference.

By the westerner, the swift decision made by one person or small group and then rapidly implemented is frequently applauded. To the Japanese the decision-making process is often more important than the decision itself for often there will not be just one best solution to a problem. It is better to have a decision on which all are agreed than one which is decided by a few and then handed down to reluctant subordinates. This can however lead to the lowest common denominator solution being accepted and, perhaps, this is one reason why the Japanese are not regarded as major innovators – although maybe this is another piece of western defensive stereotyping!

Japanese meetings may, to the westerner, often seem to be unstructured and over-concerned with trivia. They range over many topics in addition to those planned. Western-type conclusions may not emerge and the meeting may end with a general affirmation of the shared values of the group. The purpose of a Japanese meeting is not, however, always to reach a decision but to share information. The mood of the meeting may be changed by looking at an issue in many different ways and what may be trivial to one particular individual may not be so to another. Even when the outcome is obvious, the discussion process may serve to educate not only others but the proposer himself.

Rarely, however, is there vigorous open debate at such meetings and in particular the senior man present is not directly challenged on his views – a reflection of the Japanese respect for seniority. To debate openly is, to many Japanese, impolite or rude and can disturb the very important internal harmony. Because the meeting may not be directed towards a firm conclusion, however, it will be open to the dissenter to indicate in an oblique way that he does have a contrary opinion and following the meeting he will have the opportunity of expressing his views privately – either directly or by using a go-between. In a western meeting directed towards a conclusion, the dissenter who does not speak up has missed the opportunity.

The concept of harmony extends also to the formal relationships between employer and employee. The main characteristic of such relationships is well known – that Japanese unions are based on the enterprise. While there are several federations, such as the General Council of Trade Unions and the Japanese Confederation of Labour, the individual unions are enterprise-based. In Japanese thinking this is linked with the lifetime employment and seniority systems whereby management and employees (and hence their union) are committed to the success of the enterprise. Thus, while there will inevitably be some differences of opinion, the areas which unite are stronger than those which divide.

This system of enterprise unions, while culturally acceptable to the Japanese, is based very much on the efforts of the American forces after the second World War, when General MacArthur was anxious to re-establish Japanese industry as a bulwark against Communism. Like the re-establishment of German trade unions it owes much to the occupying forces (the late General Secretary of the TUC, Vic Feather, was always proud of his contribution towards establishing industry-based unions in Germany), and under MacArthur, union membership peaked at more than 50 per cent in the late 1940s. Today, it is less than 30 per cent.

But the concept of enterprise-based unions is heavily criticized by traditional western unions, and it is easy to put onto the system an interpretation of 'unions being in the managements' pocket'. Enterprise unions can, however, only be really judged in relation to the total Japanese ethos, where, because of lifetime employment etc. the Japanese worker sees his long-term prosperity bound up with that of the company. Trade Union officials will oppose the company but sometimes their membership will say they have gone too far. Ichiro Shiogi, President of the Nissan Auto Workers Union, vigorously opposed the establishment of the company's UK investment, often against the wishes of his membership, who accepted the company's desire to invest overseas. Although a complex affair, this opposition was partly the cause of his being forced to resign two years after the final decision was made.

Full-time union officials are often company employees, seconded by the company to the union following their election. At a time when relationships between the company and the union are good such a move can be beneficial to the career of a promising executive, particularly if he works enthusiastically for the mutual benefit of the union and the company. On the manual side of the union, more than 50 per cent of full time officials in the Nissan Union – and this is typical – are foremen. In such an environment, for a worker to go on strike is now somewhat unusual. In 1984 only 354 000 man days were lost due to strikes, although in the 1970s Japan ranked 14th among industrial nations and had a worse strike record than Holland and Germany. During pay negotiations, which are often very tough, solidarity is demonstrated by wearing an armband or headband. Sometimes, banners will be displayed or meetings held out of working hours. Very occasionally overtime will be banned for a short period but the lost production will be made up by harder work the following day. The basic increase is then negotiated at the very top level with the Company and Union Presidents sitting together – the people who make the decisions are in the front line. There is nothing similar to the western concept of keeping the top men in reserve in case of breakdown. When all are committed to the corporate goal real breakdowns simply do not occur and what the Union does not want to do is to price the company out of the market. Within the closed labour market your personal future is tied to the future of your company – if the company goes down you go with it.

It is common when comparing the efficiency of various countries to say something like 'They don't actually work harder – they are just more efficient'. This is only part of the truth. In the words of Nissan's *Things you want to know about Nissan and Japan* 'Even with the latest equipment and technologies, a high level of productivity cannot be achieved without a high quality workforce. Japanese workers apply themelves industriously and earnestly to their assigned tasks, excel at teamwork and take pride in maintaining good attendance records.' Whether or not this gives satisfaction is a different question. Most older Japanese executives will point to a reducing commitment to work. A Prime Minister's Office survey found in 1980 that only 20 per cent of workers aged between 20 and 24 found satisfaction in work, compared to 29 per cent in 1971. This was not only a significant reduction, but a surprisingly low figure in relation to the general perception of Japanese commitment. This view was reinforced by a 1986 survey of loyalty to the company, conducted by the Japanese Federation of Electrical Machinery Workers.[9] Covering 11 000 workers in nine countries, the Japanese ranked eighth when considering the degree of satisfaction with working life (measured over 20 factors). They came behind Great Britain, West Germany, Italy, Sweden, Hungary, Poland, Yugoslavia and Hong Kong. Sweden was at the top.

Japanese offices, unlike the production areas, are overmanned according to Western standards and the level of computerisation is very low – perhaps due to the difficulty of obtaining sophisticated software. There is a common perception that Japanese workers stay for long hours 'in case they are wanted'. This is certainly not true in production areas but is so, relative to western standards, in the offices. Many do in fact go home immediately after working hours – witness the evening rush hour which is not significantly different to the morning's. However, many others do wait until the senior man leaves before they go, but often the time between the normal finish and actual leaving time will not be totally productive. This can also be used as a pretext for the incapable men to cover up their inefficiencies. The fact is, however, that Japanese do work longer hours. In 1980, when Japanese working hours averaged 2108 per year, the Labour Ministry set a five-year target to reduce to 2000 hours. In 1984 actual hours had risen to 2116. American and West European hours ranged in the same year from 1700 to 1900 hours a year.

The actual working pattern in Japan normally includes a half day on Saturdays, although in the last few years there has been pressure to *schedule* alternate Saturdays as days off, which is not the same as meaning that they are actually *taken* off. Some 70 per cent of small Japanese firms (less than 300 employees) remain on a six day week according to a survey by the National Federation of Small Business Associations and there has been no change in the number of six-day workers since 1974. Annual vacation in the blue chip companies is normally three weeks, but frequently this is not all taken, for commitment to the company means that some of the holiday should not be used. Sickness is often recorded as vacation, so that an employee, taking a few days off for a minor illness, will normally have his holiday reduced by the corresponding amount. A US Embassy Report *Labor Trends in Japan*[10] states 'Workers in 1981 used only 55 per cent or 8.3 days of their annual leave entitlement of 15 days'.

Japanese business is concerned with the whole person. The Nissan publication states 'The company welfare system in Japan provides for such basic benefits as uniforms, food and housing as well as for the individual's personal life, in the areas of leisure, education and culture. From family housing to cultural, athletic and recreational facilities to company financed insurance, these benefits are designed to provide employees with an environment in which they can fully realise their abilities, and to maintain and improve their well-being outside the workplace itself'. This policy also includes medical care and means that 'blue chip' companies often have their own small hospitals with amazingly sophisticated facilities for carrying out both treatment and operations. While developed from the post-World War II privations, this commitment of the company to its workforce is but a logical extension of the mediaeval lord-vassal relationships.

While it can be argued that it ties the worker to the employer, this view totally misinterprets the basic nature of the relationship.

This relationship is not only demonstrated between the employee and the company but also between the employee and his foreman. Often described as an older to younger brother relationship, the foreman is expected to develop a genuine interest in the welfare of his workers. Thus, if a Japanese employee is sick, the foreman will visit him, not to check up to see if he is genuinely ill, but out of an interest in his well-being. Such a relationship in the office is less welcomed, although in one particular aspect it remains very strong. When a junior wishes to marry he will normally ask his superior to assist – not by finding a bride but by acting as a matchmaker in discussions with the two families and by checking out the suitability of the arrangement. At the actual wedding, the top table will consist of the bride and groom plus the matchmaker and his wife. The principal guests will normally be senior staff in the company.

The purpose of this chapter has been twofold. First to determine those elements of Japanese management practices which are not transferable in their stereotyped form to a western culture, and second to show that the stereotype is not always accurate. Dr Ian Gow, Director of the Japanese Business Policy Unit at Warwick University, has denigrated the tendency of western managers to take the short cut to understanding Japan, by which route Tokyo is 'magically transformed into a sort of industrial Lourdes for the battered and ailing industries of the west'. In an excellent summation of the problem of the instant solution, Dr Gow continues 'unfortunately much of the knowledge gathered has been rather superficial and stereotyped; excellent fare for the faddist managers, those with a 'quick fix' mentality susceptible to consultant-driven panaceas. In truth we have only an idealised, often out-of-date, sanitised version of Japanese-style management based on constantly recycled versions of the human resource and other management techniques of some of Japan's larger companies. Such literature does scant justice to the richness and complexity of the varied forms of Japanese management and inadequately examines their weaknesses, particularly in regard to their human and other costs'.[11]

There is, however, much we can learn from the Japanese. In Nissan we have been fortunate because many of our staff have received much more than the superficial, sanitised version of

Japanese management practices. We have spent months working on the shop floor alongside Japanese workers and have been supervised by Japanese foremen and managers. We have been on the receiving end of the practical manifestations of the much vaunted philosophy and thus have begun to achieve an *understanding* of that philosophy.

We have concluded that much that is good about Japanese management practices *is* transferable, with modification, to a western environment. Indeed, those elements which *are* transferable can almost be regarded as 'international' rather than 'Japanese'. This concept is also reflected by Wilson

> managers have gone crazy in the past decades; trying to follow the Japanese mode, in the hope of emulating Japan's industrial success. The way the Japanese manage their factories has two distinct ingredients, one spilling out of their traditions, which western societies cannot hope to replicate; the other judiciously imported from America and Europe at an earlier stage – and that, having first appeared in the West, does not need to be recopied from Japan. The particular amalgam in Japanese enterprises, of Japanese social groupism with western systems of organising industrial production, is too varied to constitute a general mode for other countries to mimic ... What could profitably be applied by Western managers is not Japan's imaginary magic formula for industrial success, but such time-worn universals as the practice of a little more care and thoroughness, a lifting of sights to the slightly longer term, a greater consideration for the self-esteem of employees.[12]

As the result of our internal analysis within Nissan we have developed our own transfer list – our tripod – Flexibility, Quality Consciousness and Teamworking. Like all tripods it is indivisible and interdependent – lose one leg and the structure falls. These three legs combined with common terms and conditions can be major determinants of success for any company. They are by no means unique to Japan but are practised in Japan to a greater extent than anywhere else. They *are*, with modification, transferable and the next three chapters, the core of this book, are concerned with the tripod. Many companies in various ways have started down this route and it is this variety of experience that is important.

3 Flexibility – the 1980s' Variety

It was in July 1966 that the government first imposed a statutory pay freeze, which lasted for the remainder of that year. The first half of 1967 was a period of 'severe restraint' with a zero norm for pay increases. From July 1968, the government allowed no automatic increases and gave itself the power to delay any increases for seven months. However, it was during this period that two exceptions were allowed – increases could be granted where low pay could be demonstrated and where productivity improvements were negotiated. For the next decade, on and off, productivity improvements became significant in justifying pay increases and were still around in the guise of 'self-financing productivity schemes' during the death throes of formal incomes policy in 1978.

With both companies and trade unions trying to find ways of paying employees more money, this period became the decade of the phoney productivity deal. Probably very few were intended to be total deceptions but in many cases, once the deal had been completed and the training exercise undertaken, the will to actually make the change happen was often not there – at least not on the shop floor, where it really mattered. One specific example, in which the author was directly involved – and which was repeated many thousands of times throughout the country – was a plumber-millwright amalgamation. Very careful analyses of the jobs were prepared, the skills highlighted and written up, each plumber was trained in those millwrighting skills he lacked and each millwright in the plumbing skills, ticks were put in boxes to show that the training in each module had taken place and at the end of it a multi-skilled craftsman with a higher rate of pay emerged. Unfortunately, but understandably, the foreman knew that the experienced plumbers were better at plumbing and the experienced millwrights better at millwrighting, so he gave each task to the person most likely to do it properly. Very little cross-fertilisation actually emerged. Anyway, the trade union attitude was often that if it did not really happen it could always be sold again at a later date!

In some areas this attitude has remained. In 1984, an IDS Study *Craft Flexibility* commented 'We also came across widespread scepticism (within and without the companies concerned) about the extent to which agreements on paper would really result in changes in practice. Even where the increased craft flexibility has been agreed in return for substantial improvements in pay and conditions, some managers told us of trade union pressure to revert to previous practice, and they admitted to concern about the abilities of some of their colleagues in line management to ensure that the agreed changes were really made and to ensure that they were adhered to'.[1]

In other areas the development of new technology, combined with the harsh economic realities of business life in the 1980s, has however brought about a sea change in attitude. Both management and trade unions are now very much more meaningful about actually achieving improvements in flexibility. The *AEU Journal* stated in 1984 'But for anyone asking themselves where the new work will be in manufacturing industry during the next decade, the answer is plain enough. It will be among the branches of engineering, which are already based in electronics and information technology, or which are capable of moving in that direction. So for people who have grown up with traditional mechanical work, and that includes most of the two and a half million strong population of British engineering, the great issue is whether the change over is possible or impossible, easy or difficult'.[2]

The second largest craft union, the EETPU, is also in the forefront of thinking in this, as in many areas. General Secretary, Eric Hammond, quoted in *Management Today*, stated that while in the first half of the century, traditional outlooks, structures, training and skills were compatible with the needs of the economy, today 'Technology has exploded on these old structures of status and pay, both between and within crafts. Production, process and craft pay differentials, which largely reflected the old levels of skills, have now become outdated'.[3] In its brochure, setting itself out as the only union which has really come to terms with the need for change, the EETPU states 'technological progress is vital to industrial survival ... Our concern is to ensure that it is successfully harnessed, not fearfully rejected by the industrial backwoodsmen in some shortsighted emotional spasm ... Productive, profitable and competitive employers offer better rewards and more long term job security for their workforces than those who stick to old fashioned methods and products'.[4]

While the immediate catalyst to this new attitude has been a combination of technological change and recession there does appear to be a genuine attempt on the part of some managements and unions to bring about a change. In his response to the 1983 CSEU claim for a 35-hour working week and a six week annual holiday, the Director General of the Engineering Employers Federation, Dr James McFarlane, said 'We need to make maximum use of plant and machinery by eliminating restrictive manning practices, by having full flexibility between and within trades and occupations and between supervisor and supervised. We need to build on our new training agreements by accepting training at any age and entry into skilled occupations, so that people can achieve their full potential ... In order to make better use of plant and equipment our member companies need to be able to adopt flexible working times when required'. The trade union response to this came in 1986 when the CSEU stated that it would be prepared to recommend to constituent unions that they cooperate with employers in eliminating demarcations and other restrictive practices in exchange for a reduction in the working week. This approach was subsequently confirmed by only a single vote majority out of 25 cast in the CSEU Executive. With the position complicated by revised bargaining procedure proposals, only the representatives of the AEU and EETPU voted in favour. However it is clear that both management and some trade unions are making the right sort of noises not because they see it as a way around government incomes policy, but because it is in their mutual interest to survive. It is, however, at plant level that the real change has to take place and this requires a considerable effort on the part of all concerned to overcome traditional attitudes and practices, established relativities and differentials, and the lethargy which makes it more comfortable to stay as we are rather than change.

Nevertheless, many companies are moving in the direction of greater flexibility among manual workers, and for the majority this time it is *real* flexibility and *real* improvements in productivity. This is not, of course, always due to enlightenment. Many of the companies, responding to the 1984 IDS Study, reported that 'the weakening of the trade unions' bargaining power has been a crucial element in their ability to bring about greater craft flexibility than before'. Other factors include the not unnatural desire for craftsmen to learn the new skills and then enhance their earning potential, either with their present employer or with another. Companies, faced with increasingly sophisticated equipment and systems, which must be effectively and efficiently maintained if they are to produce at their optimum level, must have their own highly skilled flexible workforce capable of undertaking most of the tasks without having to rely on other individuals or outsiders.

It is not only at the craft level that companies are seeking flexibility. Traditionally, British industry has created rigid demarcations between the skilled and non-skilled employee, although once he leaves the factory the 'non-skilled' person may often perform a range of tasks at home, on the car or on a voluntary basis which, if done at work, would result in a dispute. It has frequently been said by shop stewards that managements fail to fully utilise the talents of their workforce. While this is no doubt true, the trade unions have been the first to prevent this flexibility, but rarely in the past has management sought to change the practice. This also is changing, although at a slower pace than multi-skilling the craftsmen. There can be no doubt, however, that the general worker is capable of undertaking a far wider range of tasks and as the craftsman becomes increasingly skilled and almost certainly more expensive, it will become inappropriate to use him on work that is well within the compass of the people actually operating the machines. Managements will therefore, in the near future, have to transfer their attention to this area of flexibility and, especially where they have a mix of unions, will find this a more difficult nut to crack than multi-skilling the craftsmen. However, in the vast majority of companies, craftsmen form only a small proportion of the workforce, and while an improvement in craftsmen efficiency can have a disproportionate effect on overall efficiency, by far the greatest gains can be made by maximising flexibility in the production areas.

It is easy to lose sight of the fact that common terms and conditions of employment means just that – there is no distinction between employees. So that if an agreement on flexibility applies to craft workers, it also applies to non-craft workers – and supervisors, administrators, engineers and managers. The wording of the Continental–TGWU agreement (closely mirrored, subsequently, by Nissan) contained certain general principles (discussed more fully in Chapter 6) and in line with the general objective 'to ensure the continuing prosperity of the Company and its employees' both parties agreed a section on Working Practices which stated:

(a) To ensure the fullest use of plant, equipment and manpower as stated in Paragraph 1 of this Agreement there will be complete flexibility and mobility of employees within their capabilities as required by the Company.

(b) It is recognised that efficient operations are not dependent on fixed manning levels and absences will not therefore be automatically covered. Each case will be decided on its merits.

(c) It is recognised that in order to remain competitive and thus ensure security of employment changes in technology, production processes etc. will be introduced and that such changes may affect both productivity and manning levels...

(d) To ensure complete flexibility of operations, employees will undertake, and/or will undertake training for, all occupations as required by the Company...

For Nissan, flexibility as one of the three legs of the tripod, was emphasised in our advertising and explained in our recruitment literature; it was covered in detail at all stages of the hiring process and extracts from the Agreement were sent with all offer letters. If candidates were not prepared to be flexible, they had every opportunity of withdrawing, and if the selectors discerned reticence on the part of the candidates, they were likely to be rejected.

The Agreement with the AEU is very clear on flexibility – it was, as far as the Company was concerned, one of the bedrocks on which future success would be built, and it permeates all aspects of the Company and its philosophy. The actual wording of the Agreement is very similar to Continental's:

(a) To ensure the fullest use of facilities and manpower, there will be complete flexibility and mobility of employees.

(b) It is agreed that changes in technology, processes and practices will be introduced and that such changes will affect both productivity and manning levels.

(c) To ensure such flexibility and change, employees will
    undertake and/or undertake training for all work as required
    by the Company. All employees will train other employees as
    required.

To adapt the sporting phrase 'There's no point in changing a
successful formula'.

What exactly do we mean by flexibility? Certainly not moving
people rapidly from section to section for that detracts from team
working. It operates at a number of different levels, but can be
summarised as 'expanding all jobs as much as possible and by
developing the capabilities of all employees to the greatest extent
compatible with efficiency and effectiveness'. To maximise
flexibility, Nissan considered it necessary to have the absolute
minimum number of job titles. In studying the tasks performed
in the motor industry in the UK, we became more and more
convinced that the British motor industry had got it wrong. Until
its 1985/86 negotiations, Ford had 516 different manual worker
job titles (now reduced to 52). In Nissan we believed that *all*
manual tasks within a car plant could be covered by two job
titles, 'Manufacturing Staff' and 'Technicians'. Nissan's manufacturing operation in Smyrna, Tennessee, had proved this possible
by establishing only two manual worker job titles – Production
Technician and Maintenance Technician – but in addition in the
UK, we determined that we would have no job descriptions,
which serve only to limit what people do rather than expand
their level of flexibility and capability. At manufacturing staff
level, this means expanding the job as much as possible.

While people are trained in a number of specific production
tasks flexibility goes much further – manufacturing staff in
NMUK have total responsibility for the quality of work they
produce. We do not employ vast numbers of In-process Inspectors, as is the norm in the UK, for if you do, the attitude develops
that 'If I don't get it right it will be picked up'. Within Nissan each
member of the manufacturing staff is expected to validate the
quality of his own work and not pass on unacceptable quality to
the next stage of the process. 'Right first time' means just that – it
is not a glib phrase to which only lip service is paid.

Nissan manufacturing staff are responsible for their own
housekeeping and keeping their area clean and painted. Japanese plants do not employ vast armies of janitors and again, as with

quality, the philosophy is to give responsibility to the individual doing the job. If the man on the line is responsible for keeping it clean, he will be far less inclined to make it dirty in the first place. One of the problems in a British car plant is of people throwing things into cars when passing down the production line. All such items – sweet wrappers, paper, etc., have to be cleaned out, and again inefficiencies are created.

Perhaps the most important element of flexibility in Japan relates to maintenance. Many assembly workers handle routine preventive maintenance and minor breakdowns, and in many cases will help the maintenance craftsman if it is necessary for him to come along. Perhaps the most significant comment made to me during a visit to Japan was by a foreman during a lengthy discussion on working practices. In response to a question on what his people did if they could not fix a breakdown and the maintenance people arrived, he answered 'Obviously they will help the maintenance man – they know more about that particular part of the job than anyone else'. Following a retranslation, I observed that there was nothing *obvious* about it. In the UK, if there is a breakdown, it *will be* necessary for the maintenance men to handle it, and it will be normal for the production workers to leave the job to return only when the problem is solved. In Japan, not only do some production personnel work with the maintenance men, but those who cannot (too many cooks spoil the broth) will work on process sheets, quality charts, problem solving etc.

In the UK, the maintenance men generally regard it as an erosion of their skills if an unskilled man is seen as being able to contribute, and the semi-skilled have little incentive to increase their responsibilities. Indeed, both management and trade unions tend to discourage this expansion. But in NMUK flexibility goes further than this, for the craftsman, when he comes along, is himself multi-skilled – or at least is undertaking a training programme, which will result in genuine multi-skilling. Beyond the need to work safely, there need be no limitations on the range of tasks employees can perform, although it has to be recognised that not everyone has the same capabilities. Training programmes for the craftsmen of the future have to take this requirement into account from the very start. Those which still retain the single craft approach are preparing young people for a limited career.

Flexibility, however, goes further. Under the process known as *kaizen* – continuous improvement Nissan seeks to create an environment in which *all* staff can contribute to improving quality, safety and productivity as a normal part of their job. This means fully involving employees in the change process so that as far as possible the person who originates an idea sees it all the way through to completion. This may result in the individual concerned preparing a drawing, rewriting a process sheet and actually undertaking the physical change. The Nissan body construction shop is now considerably different from the original layout and the vast majority of these changes have been thought up and implemented by the people working in the area. In many environments management fights to introduce change whereas in the Nissan environment the individual 'owns' the change and the problem is not introducing change but keeping up with the proposals.

Many other of the greenfield site agreements have introduced flexibility as a basic element. At Inmos, the company and the EETPU support the principle and practice of 'complete flexibility of jobs and duties for all employees, both within and between departments'. Findus, at Long Benton outside Newcastle, agreed with the AEU and GMB that:

> In order to fully utilise manpower resources, all employees will perform work within their skills and capability. To achieve this, individuals will accept any necessary training and be prepared to move from job to job as the needs of the operation require.

This means both craft interchangeability and, among process grades, complete flexibility on process work plus some overlap with the traditional craft tasks. In what was the first of the famous EETPU agreements with Japanese electronics companies, it was agreed with Toshiba that:

> the trade union recognises and supports the complete flexibility of jobs and duties within the company, both within departments and between the various departments of the company, subject to individual skills and capabilities. In return the company recognises and accepts the need for training and retraining in the broadening of skills and in new technological developments, as they affect the company's efficiency as a manufacturing operation.

Significantly, these agreements, and others like them, are couched in general terms. There are no minutely detailed agreements on which trade will specifically do which particular aspects of another trade. Once you have an agreement, which provides for 'total flexibility', anything added on is restrictive.

Among established companies, flexibility deals are necessarily more complicated and more difficult to achieve, but many companies have made significant progress. Prompted by the introduction of a new microprocessor controlled plant requiring additional skills, Colemans of Norwich reached an agreement with five trade unions during its 1983 pay negotiations whereby in return for a higher increase in pay, the unions gave an agreement to 'achieve a skilled workforce of multi-skilled craftsmen each capable of performing complete tasks rather than being confined to individual skills'.

In 1981, Scottish and Newcastle Breweries negotiated a national 'flexibility-enabling agreement' with the TGWU, which provided for flexible working across the whole range of internal jobs, subject to the employees' being properly trained. This national enabling agreement required local discussions and agreement before a £12 per week flexibility payment was made, and as a result the first payments were made in May 1982. This agreement with the TGWU created pressure on and from the craftsmen, and as a result in January 1983, an agreement was reached with three main principles:

1. That individuals would be willing to perform agreed tasks outwith those traditionally within their trade, the only constraint being individual skill levels and competence in the area of any new tasks and their requirement to comply with the Health and Safety at Work Act 1974 and subsequent Acts or amendments, together with the regulations contained therein and any subsequent regulations.

2. That individuals will carry out work in locations or departments outwith their normal place of employment, as required.

3. That willingness to cooperate in agreed training/experience programmes is an essential pre-requisite to 1 and 2 above.

Part of a total pay and conditions package, this agreement provided for subsequent local negotiations on details prior to payment being received. Within a few months, 60 per cent of the craftworkers had reachd agreement and were being paid, but it was not until a year later, April 1984, that the final group in the Tyne Brewery reached agreement.

The 1985 agreement at Pilkington Insulation Ltd. introduced a common nine-grade salary structure encompassing all employees up to middle management level. This resulted in all employees being on spot salaries, and an agreement providing for full flexibility and mobility between tasks and departments was reached. Interestingly, the grading order was based on the Hay job evaluation system. The terms and conditions of employment were harmonised and two of the Unions – TASS and UCATT – lost recognition. Experience at Pilkington Insulation, and earlier at Pilkington's Greengate plant, served to influence significant change in 1986 at the company's Cowley Hill site – a 'brownfield' site if ever there was one. Covering among other things a unified pay structure, new grading system, craft and production flexibility and harmonisation, Pilkington belies the argument that it is one thing for greenfield sites to introduce change but it is much tougher in well established companies. That argument is usually an excuse for doing nothing! In another well established company, Babcock Power of Newbury, a two-year pay and flexibility deal was introduced in April 1985, and this also included proposals for a 'convergence' of hourly paid and staff conditions. The first year provided for flexibility across trades, but within unions, with the second year extending flexibility across union and possibly 'staff hands on manual work'. In November 1985 Ford's offer to the trade unions departed significantly from its previous approach and marked a major step towards achieving greater flexibility. Following a no-strings offer of 3 per cent, the Company offered additional awards conditional upon agreement to far-reaching changes to working practices. Under the proposals craft employees 'are required to adopt revised work practices in accordance with the following principles:

– versatility and flexibility
–the acquisition and use of new skills
–the elimination of inefficient lines of demarcation'.

Under these proposals, electrical and mechanical craftsmen 'must be flexible and versatile across the full range of their respective skills, undertake any electrical or mechanical tasks outside their own trade, subject to capability, that are necessary to complete an assignment'. There followed a comprehensive listing of additional skills the two types of craftsmen must acquire, which cumulatively have the effect of introducing radical changes in the Company's practices. For example 'Mechanical craftsmen must acquire and apply the full range of mechanical skills from all the mechanical trades and apply advanced pneumatics and hydraulic skills necessary for the maintenance of equipment, which includes such technology in its control or operating systems'.

The same general requirements were applicable to production operators (the new title for line workers). 'Operators must, if required, perform all the tasks, should process and operating conditions allow or should their operation be restructured to accommodate the whole range. Operators must also undertake any necessary training programmes. Flexibility and mobility within and between departments and operating units is essential. Operators must keep their immediate and surrounding work areas clean.' In reducing the number of job titles numerous different craft designations came together in the title of Mechanical Maintenance Craftsman and eighteen separate material handling and storekeeping job titles were combined under the title of Material Handler.

In response to Union comment, Ford denied that the plans were part of a strategy designed to introduce 'Nissan-type' working practices. While no doubt influenced by the Nissan agreements, the Ford proposals only dealt with one part of the equation. Although initially rejected by employees, a subsequent improvement to Ford's 'final offer' resulted in agreement at national level. Local discussions progressed well enough to convince the Company that the 4 per cent productivity element in the deal should be paid. Ford is now claiming a 50 per cent increase in productivity over the last two years.

The November 1985 deal between Caterpillar Tractors and the AEU significantly advanced the cause of flexibility. Reducing the 51 job titles to 12, it also provided that within each of five pay groups, flexibility will be limited only by individual capability. Specific examples included flexibility between assemblers, adjusters and testers, multi-skilling of craftsmen and cooperation on sharing job knowledge and experience. Once craftsmen became multi-skilled in both electrical and mechanical work, they received a higher rate of pay.

A less revolutionary flexibility deal has been reached at

Anglesey Aluminium (formed by Rio Tinto Zinc and Kaiser Aluminium). The relevance of this agreement, effective for eighteen months from September 1985, is not so much in what it actually achieved but as an indication that many companies in many shapes and sizes are going down this road. All any company can do is what is right for it in its own circumstances. The fact that this company – and many others – are on the move is the significant point.

Part of a larger pay and conditions package involving considerable progress to harmonisation and headcount reductions, the Anglesey Aluminium agreement with the EETPU and ASTMS provided for increased flexibility 'between the various craft descriptions and across the traditional craft/semi-skilled boundary', subject to a number of principles. These principles maintain that the prime responsibility of individual craftsmen is to their base craft and that they will only work outside their base craft when it is necessary to progress the job in hand. They will not be directed to a job, which lies outside their primary skill, unless they have had adequate training. 'Where it is agreed that these principles have been met, then flexibility will be applied accordingly'. It is also agreed that 'in the interests of the most efficient operation of the plant, work not requiring specialist craft skills can be carried out by any employee who has been given the necessary training'.

This agreement is very much an enabling agreement, and its success will depend on the willingness of the parties to take positive steps forward. There can be little doubt, however, that in the atmosphere of the 1980s, the will for real change is much greater than during the incomes policy era, when such measures were no more than devices to give employees more money for little return.

Even the most traditional areas of British industry are not immune. Vickers and Cammell Laird at Birkenhead, Merseyside, following their 1986 privatisation negotiated a comprehensive package with the CSEU. Not only does this package include a commitment to achieving complete harmonisation by 1989 but also an agreement, seen as an initial step, which states:

It is understood and accepted that flexibility shall be where an employee carries out tasks which are normally associated with other trades in order to progress his own work within the limits of his own competence and utilising the appropriate tools and equipment. No prior notification will be required for implementation of flexibility, as it shall be an ongoing procedure.

There then follows a number of specifics which put flesh on the bones of the general agreement. It is somewhat salutory to think that this agreement, negotiated between the CSEU and the management consortium which bought out the company from the public sector, might, if reached ten years earlier by the same people, have gone some way towards alleviating many of the problems of the shipbuilding industry. While not resolving the world overcapacity situation, it could have put the British yards in a better position to compete in the changed market place. Still, that is the story of British industry.

In recognition of these changes, the CBI delivered a paper to the NEDC in January 1986 emphasising that the movement to greater flexibility was 'no short lived response to recession'. The CBI reported that in a sample survey of its members, 57 per cent expected to reduce demarcation and increase multi-skilling and flexibility over the next five years. It found no-one moving in the opposite direction. A not unexpected result!

The fact that there is so much comment on those companies which have made progress in increasing flexibility serves only to emphasise that most have a long way to go. In its most recent survey of the subject, *Flexibility at Work*, IDS commented, 'With very few exceptions, the process of achieving full scale flexibility has hardly begun. There are exceptions ... but in general progress has been limited. The gap between the advanced companies and the large majority is considerable'.[5]

As a result of its analysis, the IDS Study made a number of other interesting observations. 'Many of the agreements are enabling agreements, which establish the possibility of change – the real tests are in the future'. Very importantly 'Real change depends on consent and commitment from all concerned'. While not expressing its objectives in this way, the whole Nissan approach of achieving employee commitment can only help this process, but then, as in many areas, the different aspects become mutually reinforcing – flexibility gives rise to responsibility, to commitment, to innovation, to quality, to pride, to flexibility and hopefully a continuation upwards in virtuous spiral.

IDS gets to the kernel when it says 'Real flexibility involves a commitment to continual change in response to the pressures of competition and rapid changes in technology. It does not require a 'one-off' set of changes, but the ability to respond to changing needs over a period'.[6] It is comparatively easy to establish the one-off change, but very much more difficult to develop the attitude that continuous improvement is essential. This is what the Japanese call *kaizen* – continuous improvement, which depends on attitude much more than what is written in a specific flexibility deal. As one manager puts it 'If you have to specify the detail of your flexibility arrangements in an agreement, you haven't got flexibility, and you are not going to get it'. Of course for most the ideal is, in the short term unattainable, but it should not be forgotten that when something is written down, those points which are not included are, by definition, excluded.

The IDS view, that most companies have a long way to go, is echoed in an Institute of Manpower Studies Report *Changing work patterns – how companies achieve flexibility to meet new needs*[7]. Commenting that most respondents were doubtful that there had been a permanent shift in attitude on the part of employees they felt that changes in bargaining strength had been the most significant factor. Further, they found that any shifts were largely limited to manufacturing rather than retail distribution or financial services, but even in manufacturing, advances were limited. Only 15 per cent had achieved dual-skilling between electrical and mechanical crafts. Very few companies had achieved flexibility across boundaries – between craft and non-craft occupations – union demarcation and training problems being most frequently cited as the reasons for lack of progress. No mention is made of flexibility between manual and non-manual workers and this is a significant omission.

But flexibility does not simply mean flexibility between manual workers. In Nissan, we have developed the concept that there are no restrictions – this can be as informal as managers shifting furniture, spending long periods in the production areas and filing their own papers to more formal arrangements for moving between jobs. Thus, in a situation in which, for example, there was an insufficient number of line workers to man the production areas, we would expect indirect workers to help out. If this meant a material handler working on production, we would expect a white-collar worker, properly trained, to do the material handler's job. Once you start on the path to flexibility, there is no logical limit, other than the fact that the cost of training everyone to do everything is disproportionate to the benefits. If managers are not flexible, however, you cannot expect people on the shop floor to respond.

To put a theoretical framework on to this concept of flexibility there are two elements in work, the prescribed and the discretionary. The prescribed elements are those which have to be done to survive. In motor manufacturing the manufacturing staffs' prescribed elements are building a car to the right quality and in the right time. Discretionary elements are those over and above the prescribed: in Nissan's case such items as self-inspection, housekeeping, maintenance, continuous improvement, and so on. The objective must be to have the prescribed elements undertaken as effectively as possible and expand the discretionary elements.

The essential point is, within the obvious constraints of the job, to maximise the areas of discretion. The vast majority of people prefer to have an influence over what they do, but when the prescribed task is essentially repetitive job satisfaction can come from performing those tasks well but even more so from influencing *how* they are done. The more influence a person can have on his environment the better. Of course nothing is static, tasks which start off as discretionary can move into the prescribed, albeit to a lower level of prescription, and new tasks can take their place.

The movement towards greater flexibility does of course have its opponents. Vociferous on the left is the Centre for Alternative Industrial and Technological Systems based at the North London Polytechnic. A booklet published by the Centre has stated that 'the attack on job security, conditions and trade union organisation contained within flexibility represents the most serious challenge to trade unionism for decades'.[8] The booklet's descriptions of Nissan's practices, while often inaccurate, attempts to denigrate the movement towards flexibility and team working and regards much of Nissan's philosophy as anti-union. Nothing could be further from the truth – unless you believe that providing people with fulfilling, meaningful jobs is anti-union. Perhaps the opponents would rather the companies remained un-competitive and the employment conditions of the staff – the union members – went downhill. At least then the militants would have something to complain about!

It would appear, however, that such criticism is limited to the more left wing sections of the trade union movement. The realities of life are well recognised by mainstream trade unionists. While they may not always be happy with the pace of change and are, of course, protective of jobs, the attitude is moving from one of resisting change to one of negotiating change and getting the best deal they can for their members. This is a perfectly legitimate response. Indeed, an internal TUC document, circulated to all trade unions in October 1986, states 'by giving workers increased responsibility for quality and output, job satisfaction can increase. By weakening job demarcation lines, jobs can get more interesting. It is important for the unions to acknowledge this and not be seen to be opposed to it'. We hope we will come to the time when trade unions not only react, but initiate. It is then that reluctant managements will have *real* problems.

4 Numerical Flexibility –
A Fashionable Theory

Flexibility does not solely relate to the work people actually do but also to the number of those employed to do it. Of course, there is nothing new in this phenomenon, particularly with regard to part-time workers in some industries and temporary workers in others. In the food industry, the hiring of temporary and/or part-time workers has been the traditional way of life. In secretarial and administrative areas numerous agencies owe their livelihood to their ability to provide an endless stream of 'temps' to work in city offices and this pattern can be repeated in many different sectors. However, it is clear that the actual pattern of employment is now shifting in a much more fundamental way and is beginning to affect manufacturing industry now as never before.

For example in the year to October 1985, two thirds of the jobs filled by the MSC Northern Region Job Centres were for full time workers and one third for part-timers. Nationally the trend to flexible working is pronounced. According to figures released by the Department of Employment in February 1987, the flexible labour force (part-timers, temporaries, home workers and self employed) accounted for 34 per cent of the total workforce in 1985 against 30 per cent in 1981 (8.12 million against 6.97 million). During this same period full-time permanent employees fell by over one million (16.64 million down to 15.61 million) – a reduction of six per cent.

The growth of temporary workers is also pronounced. An Institute of Manpower Studies survey, reported in the *Employment Gazette*,[1] suggested that traditionally the three factors that cause fluctuations in temporary working are now all working in a positive direction. These factors are the economic cycle, structural change (towards the service sector) and new manning practices aimed at greater flexibility. Thus, the survey showed that since 1980, 39 per cent of employers have increased their use of temporary staff against 17 per cent who have reduced, (44 per cent were unchanged). It was the larger and growing organisations which were mainly responsible for this increase.

Over half of the temporaries are employed in the traditional occupations, such as catering and cleaning, but growth is clearly expected in professional and other non-manual occupations. However, as significant, were what the IMS Study refers to as 'new reasons' for employing temporary staff. Included in those 'new reasons' were a number associated 'with being more flexible in the face of uncertainty and volatility'. Often such attitudes are portrayed as employers trying to save both recruitment and employment costs, but, says IMS, 'few employers claimed to be motivated by a wish to save on direct recruitment and employment costs through the use of temporary workers.... Case study employers generally argued that the advantages of being able to match manning levels precisely to workloads and the extra flexibility gained from being able to adjust the size of the workforce rapidly without incurring major severance costs, exceeded any advantages due to lower wage and non-wage costs of using temporaries'. These new reasons were associated more with employers who were increasing their use of temporary workers rather than by those decreasing their use.

Explaining this, several of the manufacturing companies argued that in climbing out of a recession they did not wish to overcommit to a permanent workforce. 'Hence in the recovery, and faced with an increase in demand (of uncertain magnitude and duration), such employers had resolved first, to consolidate the productivity gains of recent years, and where possible, meet such demands with the existing workforce: second, where recruitment is essential, to take temporary workers in the first instance, who can be shed at short notice.' It is partly because of this that most companies pay little attention to the training of their temporary workers; they are generally placed in low skill content tasks or where any skills are of a general transferable nature.

Such is the movement and subsequent change in company structures, that the process is attracting the attention of the academics. To the forefront of these is John Atkinson of the Institute of Manpower Studies at the University of Sussex, who presented his theories in a paper 'Flexibility: planning for an uncertain future'.[2] John Atkinson distinguishes between numerical flexibility, functional flexibility and financial flexibility. Functional flexibility covers the tasks performed within a working environment, as discussed earlier, but numerical flexibility is concerned with 'the ease with which the number of workers employed can be adjusted to meet fluctuations in the level of demand'. The fluctuations might be short or long, predictable or unpredictable. 'But whatever the fluctuation looks like, the numerically flexible firm is the one which always deploys exactly the right number of workers at each stage of the fluctuation rather than suffering shortages at one point or overmanning at another.' (Financial flexibility encourages and supports the other two.)

John Atkinson's flexible firm consists of a core group of employees surrounded by peripheral groups, who may or may not be employees, sub-contractors, specialist self-employed workers, perhaps on fee-based, short-term contracts, agency temporaries and trainees. A second group may include employees, who are on one of the government job creation schemes – public subsidy trainees or jobsharers – or people on temporary contracts or employed on arrangements designed to bring them to work only when required.

It is at the centre that John Atkinson's 'core' group of employees lies and it is these who are most required to deliver the functional flexibility, for it is clearly not possible to employ temporary workers on the full range of skills developed by the 'core' group. It is a mistake, however, to believe that non-core personnel are less skilled, for in many cases they may have a skill which is rare but not in frequent demand – many of the specialist subcontractors fall into this category. But as John Atkinson states 'relatively few UK firms have explicitly and comprehensively reorganised their labour force on this basis. While most are certainly drifting in this direction, their manpower policies and thinking tend to be dominated by pragmatism and opportunism'.

Some companies are however making specific moves in this direction. The original Continental Can–TGWU agreement made no mention of part time, casual or temporary workers, but it quickly became evident that there was a need for such groups of staff to cope with the fluctuations of a seasonal trade and to handle some of the regular but not necessarily full time requirements. Thus, after the 1983 job evaluation exercise, a specific category of Temporary Worker was introduced. Another company to recognise its need to increase the use of temporary labour, is Caterpillar Tractor, which included a reference in its 1985 deal negotiated with the AEU. Under this agreement, up to 10 per cent of the manual workforce may be employed on temporary contracts of between six and twelve months duration. If the number looks as though it will exceed 10 per cent, an equivalent number will be transferred to permanent status on the basis of seniority. In addition, once a temporary employee has been with the company for more than twelve months, he or she automatically becomes permanent.

One company which did set out to determine its flexible manning strategy, Control Data, has had to revise its practice. Writing in *Manpower Policy and Practice*, Roger Leek, Control Data's Personnel Manager, stated 'The initial attempts to change attitudes to employment patterns were, perhaps, too fast to carry the majority of the workforce along with the concept'.[3] The company introduced a ten-month supplemental contract for new hires. Towards the end of this period the company's financial position was reviewed and if corporate performance allowed, the individual was confirmed as a full-timer and joined the 'core labour force'. This arrangement worked as long as the company was expanding, but when demand began to plateau out and the supplemental contracts terminated at the ten-month period, problems began to arise. Those who were within the ten-month period, were retained and those who reached ten-months would have to leave. This conflicted with the general attitude of 'last in first out'. Management did not wish to give up the ability to control selection but, following a review, agreed a number of modifications to the system, which restricted the total numbers of supplemental employees to 15 per cent, and identified them as part timers by limiting hours to 15 per week. They were to be employed on lower-graded jobs and any short-term reduction in headcount would be managed through the supplemental employment policy. By also increasing the use of sub-contractors, standby operators and outservicing (small local companies undertaking some of the assembly work), Control Data introduced refinements, which made their strategy a close fit to John Atkinson's theoretical model. The Nissan agreement recognised from the start that the Company could usefully employ temporary staff, and included a paragraph which states: 'The Company may at its discretion hire temporary or part time employees to cope with seasonal or short term fluctuations in work levels'.

Because the year of manufacture is denoted by the prefix letter on the registration plate there is a considerable increase in the number of cars sold in the month of the change. Consequently, in the preceding months, car manufacturers need to build many more vehicles than normal to ensure that dealers are fully stocked. This can result in considerably increased overtime and a lengthening of the period during which the cars are held in storage prior to sale, with subsequent increased costs due to inventory holdings being greater than normal.

Nissan's solution to this problem is virtually unique in the British motor industry – to hire temporary workers in the months preceding the date of the registration change. In so doing, however, the company has to be mindful of the need to maintain the quality of staff, both technically and in their attitude. Thus all such candidates go through the same selection process as those originally hired. In addition, they are hired at least a month before they are actually needed, so that at least in one job they reach the required quality standard.

Obviously such people have to be unemployed at the time and, conscious of the possible accusations of exploitation, Nissan regards such appointments as a positive step towards permanent employment with the company. In fact of the first 70 temporary workers hired in 1987 the company was subsequently able to offer permanent positions to around 60. It is obvious why both individuals and unions are apprehensive about such trends, and the TUC voiced these concerns to the NEDC in December 1985. In speaking of the 'growing concentration on the notion of flexibility as applied to the labour market' it considered that for many employers 'it is merely the cloak for undermining collective rights, organisation and agreed terms and conditions'. The TUC argued that 'recent trends are best described as an overall growth in insecure forms of employment rather than any innovative or more efficient pattern'. Critical of the IMS core-periphery theory, the TUC states 'Certainly the notion that a secure and flexible "core" of workers is being created on a wide scale is undermined by the general degree of insecurity and worsening conditions being experienced by *all* groups of workers.' While the TUC was obviously making a political point, there is reality in the fears, and a responsible company should ensure that none of the worst possibilities develop in its employment of temporary staff.

It is interesting that a month later in January 1986, the CBI, in its paper delivered to the NEDC, also had a slight dig at the work of the IMS. Emphasising the importance of achieving flexibility of working practices, reducing overmanning and demarcation, the

CBI added 'This is the sort of change that can be at the heart of achieving greater labour market flexibility; and we believe that to some extent it has been obscured by the slightly tangential debate, which has developed about core and peripheral employees'.

Again, as in so many matters, the trade union movement, after initial resistance, will come to terms with this development – particularly as this one is not new. Demonstrating the concern over the growth of temporary working, the 1986 CSEU conference passed a resolution calling for 'an extensive examination of the use of temporary labour.... To examine the terms and conditions of employment ... and to develop a coherent policy for recommendation to affiliated unions'. The TGWU in December 1986 announced a recruitment drive aimed specifically at temporary workers. Said Ron Todd, 'The nature of the labour force has been changing dramatically and will continue to do so. We cannot afford to be tied to the employment patterns of yesteryear. It is our intention to take the initiative and shape events, not to sit back and let them happen'[4]

With the official launch of the campaign, known as Link-Up, being supported by Neil Kinnock it remains to be seen whether it will be successful in arresting the TGWU's membership decline which has taken it from more than 2.0 million in 1979 to 1.38 million in 1986. Emphasising the urgency of the issue, Norman Willis, speaking at the TUC Women's Conference in March 1987, called for 'another great surge of unionisation mainly, but not only in the private services... The crisis could well be terminal for those that continue down well-worn tracks and do nothing to make themselves relevant and attractive to groups of workers they have not traditionally recruited... We must find new ways of organising and representing growing categories of workers'. Temporary workers have in the past been notoriously difficult for unions to organise and most have put little effort into this sector. Whether such initiatives can have an effect on subsequent recruitment remains to be seen, but at a time when the trade union movement is struggling to retain membership it cannot ignore this significant growth area among the working population.

5 Quality – Above All

Everything you hear about the Japanese attitude to quality is true. Commitment to a zero defect product is absolute – not only at top management levels but throughout the company – particularly at the 'sharp end' where the products are actually made. Assembly workers genuinely take a pride in building the perfect product, and they insist that the components they receive are of the same high standard. They totally fail to understand the attitude prevalent in the West that quality is someone else's business – particularly the practice of employing vast numbers of Inspectors whose task it is to check the work of the assembler.

In British industry, while we pay lip service to the view that 'we must build in quality not inspect it in', it is a regular practice to employ numerous In-process Inspectors, one after each foreman's group, to check the work of that group. This leads to the attitude, 'If I don't get it right it will be picked up – and that creates a job for an inspector and a repairman'. In Japan the assembly worker has total responsibility for the quality of work he produces. Until the final checking of the vehicle at the end of each main department, individual tasks are not inspected by anyone other than the assembler.

The British philosophy often degenerates into, at best, 'We have to hit schedule but give me the right quality' and at worst can develop into a 'Numbers at any price' syndrome although, faced with overseas competition and standards, this low point in the British motor industry disappeared many years ago.

Quality has many different meanings. To many, it simply means 'does it work – does everything stay together?' To others the basic specification is important – a painted car body totally hides the sheet metal and anti-corrosion treatment and, superficially, the car is assessed on the quality of its paintwork. But that paintwork can cover a high grade or low grade steel or a comprehensive or minimal anti-corrosion process. Japanese products are celebrated for the fact that they do not go wrong, that they last a long time – and that is all about specification. The Japanese car manufacturer sets a very high specification for all components and knows that it will be achieved. He does not inspect 'goods received', for over the years he will have built up a

61

long-term relationship with a single supplier for each component, which gives him total confidence in the ability of that supplier to produce components of the required quality. He will know that the supplier's research, engineering and development, his quality assurance techniques, and the attitude of his workers are such that quality standards will be met. There simply is no risk of this not being the case.

The way the Japanese measure quality is significantly different from the British way. In the UK, manufacturers of most products measure the quality of their products at the in-house inspection stage by the cost of rectifying a fault. Thus a high cost rectification will attract a high number of demerit points. The Japanese measure quality, not only in relation to the cost of repair, but also take into account the customer's perception of a fault. Thus a fault which would be discernable to the majority of customers, would be rated far worse than a fault discernable only to the expert. The archetypal fault on a car is the loose grab handle which, while low in cost to repair, is highly visible. In Japan, though a low cost rectification, this would have the worst rating in terms of customer perception. At the earliest stage of the development of NMUK it was decided that we should adopt the Japanese method and standards. Quality is a hard point on which there can be no compromise. The standards we are measured against are exactly the same as those used in Japan and as a result quality forms a major part of NMUK human relations policies.

The Nissan Agreement with the AEU states in Paragraph One, the General Principles (which are inviolate)

> both parties are agreed on the need:
> to establish an enterprise committed to the highest levels of quality, productivity and competitiveness using modern technology and working practices and to make such changes to this technology and working practices as will maintain this position.

The Constitution of the Company Council states that it will be involved in:

> matters concerning the Company's business e.g. quality production levels, market share, profitability, investment etc.

It is no accident that 'quality' is the first item on both lists. Even more emphatically the Company's philosophy statement issued to all employees (for full discussion see Chapter 6) states in its first sentence:

'We aim to build profitably the highest quality car sold in Europe.'

It is not only at shop level that this attitude to quality is apparent – it permeates all levels and it is here that the true nature of Japanese management egalitarianism comes in. Because of their education level, the seniority system, continuous in-house training, development and rotation and sheer dedication, the general level of detailed technical knowledge of senior Japanese management far exceeds all but the very highest in Britain, the United States or Germany. NMUK recruited some of the best production and engineering management from the British motor industry and they have all been amazed at the strength of their Japanese counterparts.

Senior Japanese management do not do the job of the production people – as sometimes happens in British industry. What they do do is to spend significant periods on the shop floor – management by walking around. They give specific attention to the production process and concentrate both on quality issues and on ways of making the job easier. The attitude is that if the job is difficult quality will suffer and if quality suffers the job must be made easier. In a somewhat apocryphal story emanating from the GM–Toyota joint project in Freemont, California, a senior Japanese engineer, seeing an assembly line worker struggling with his job, spent an hour or so trying to determine how to put it right. After working out a successful solution he apologised to the operator because he, the engineer, had failed in his responsibility to make the production operation as easy as possible!

All British personnel who visited Japan became convinced that we could achieve Japanese attitudes to quality and reach, and possibly beat, Japanese standards. But how is it to be achieved? There is no one simple answer. The British do not respond to slogans exhorting greater efforts to beat quality targets. Money spent on posters seeking to persuade people to improve quality is probably even more wasted than that spent on safety posters. You cannot achieve quality by sending people on courses and most of all you cannot mouth platitudes and then do everything to demonstrate that you do not mean what you say.

To achieve real quality everyone at every level in the organisation has to genuinely believe in it and act on that belief. Management must mean what it says. As soon as a senior manager allows a car to go through which is not at the right quality level 'because I have to meet schedule' the battle is lost. Whatever he has achieved with his workforce up to that point will be dissipated and perhaps never recovered. Thus the solution starts with top management commitment and that is not something that can be taught. We discovered this commitment by working with the Japanese, absorbing their values on quality and by determining that we would show the Japanese that the British could produce to Japanese standards. In retrospect this is exactly the same process that GM management went through in their association with Toyota, as did Nissan's US plant in Smyrna, Tennessee. The fact that Bluebirds built in the UK are of as high a quality as those built in Japan is testament to the success of the NMUK approach.

Much of the Supervisor's morning meeting with his staff (see Chapter 10) is about quality, how to resolve problems and continuously improve. *Kaizen* workshops have been introduced where employees with ideas for new tooling or other changes can go to try them out. All employees (not just production) are encouraged to study the quality of the cars in the vehicle evaluation bay.

Most importantly the training system emphasises quality more than anything else. Employees are trained to achieve the required quality standard and only when they have reached this level do they progress to the standard time. All employees are trained in a variety of tasks and in some are expected to reach a standard where they are capable of training others. It is the responsibility of the Supervisor to ensure that he develops a skill matrix so that within his section each individual job can be performed at the required quality level by the majority of his team and that specific individuals have the capability of training others and trouble shooting in a more limited number of jobs.

In most British auto manufacturers a system of tag relief is operated whereby relief men are built into the group numbers and each individual is relieved in succession without the lines being stopped. In addition to the problems this creates for the foreman in trying to control relief time, it also makes it much more difficult to determine which operator was working on a particular task at a particular time. Thus, if a quality problem arises, it is not impossible to blame someone else. In Japanese plants a system of block relief is used meaning that the production lines are halted for the break period. In addition to reducing manning levels, and making the foreman's job easier, it also makes it possible to identify the source of poor workmanship should this occur. When combined with the attitude that such problems need correction rather than punishment it is easy to determine the advantages of the Japanese system over the British. Such is the pride of the Japanese worker in the job that he is often genuinely thankful when a problem is picked up, for while it is an indication that he has not been performing correctly, the desire to produce the right quality overcomes the short term concern.

Without doubt, however, Western interest in the Japanese approach to quality is mainly centred on Quality Control Circles: in simple terms the thinking goes something like 'Our quality is poor, Japanese quality is good. The Japanese have Quality Control Circles – if we introduce Quality Control Circles our quality will improve'. Nothing could be further from the truth. QCCs work in Japan because they are part of the total philosophy which puts quality first and to which everyone is committed. When they are successful they emerge almost naturally as an extension of the normal way of doing the job. To believe that QCCs can simply be introduced into the UK and be successful, without other fundamental changes in attitude, is a delusion. It is not insignificant that those British companies, which have had most success with QCCs e.g. Wedgewood, Black & Decker, Mullard (Hazel Grove) and IBM (Havant), are those whose whole management style accentuates both quality and participation. Equally some of the most celebrated failures have been where management has decreed that QCCs *will* be introduced and little else is changed.

Japan has the credit for introducing the concept of QCCs and it almost seems to the westerner that the concept is one of those that has been around for ever. QCCs did not however develop in Japan until the late 1950s – early '60s following visits to that country by two American statisticians – Dr W. E. Deming in 1950 and Dr J. J. Juran in 1954. The two gentlemen travelled around Japan demonstrating the basic concepts of statistical quality control techniques represented by control charts and statistical sampling. As these concepts were assimilated by Japanese engineers, quality control activities began in the production areas, particularly involving the foremen and it was this process which developed into the QCC activities. It took however until 1962 for the movement to reach take-off point with the first Quality Control Conference for Foremen and this was followed in 1963 by the first All Japan QC Circle Conference. The rest, as they say, is history.

It is interesting to note, however, that in the country which enthusiastically embraced the QCC concept, the purpose has always been much wider than simply quality. The Nissan document, which explains the history and development of QCC in the Company, lists the basic idea behind QCC activities 'carried out as a part of Company wide quality control activities':

1. Contribute to the improvement and development of the enterprise
2. Respect humanity and build a happy bright workshop which is meaningful to work in
3. Display human capabilities fully and eventually draw out infinite possibilities.

In fact, in general, of all projects covered by QCCs in Nissan, Japan, only around one third are concerned with quality as such. Efficiency accounts for a further third with the remaining third covering items such as cost, safety, morale, etc.

It should be remembered however that QCCs are not always successful, even in Japan. Dr Ian Gow, Director of the Japanese Business Policy Unit at Warwick University, has stated 'the use of QC Circles in Japan has been exaggerated and their failure rate there has been ignored. Generally speaking QC Circles are only introduced as a refinement once Total Quality Control has been achieved. In other words QC Circles are a fine-tuning mechanism for companies whose quality record is already very good'.[1]

In assessing the reasons for failure of QC Circles in the UK this factor and the lack of employee commitment have often been overlooked. Ron Collard and Barrie Dale[2] have listed some 20 reasons for failure. Of these 20, about three quarters can come under the heading of 'Lack of managerial interest and commitment', and of these the highest three were:

1. Circle leaders lacked time to organise meetings
2. Lack of co-operation from middle management
3. Lack of co-operation from first time supervisors

A notable absentee from the 20 reasons for failure is 'lack of commitment from top management'. Perhaps this is not surprising when it is normally top management who respond to such questionnaires. However, when turning the issue on its head and considering the conditions for successful introduction and operation of quality circles the factor which heads the list is:

> Secure the commitment of the board and senior management by explaining the objectives and seeking an understanding that commitment means providing resources for training, allowing meetings in working time and making themselves available for the presentations of circles when appropriate and all this on a long term basis.

It is strange, but not surprising, that the factor which is at the head of the list making for success, is entirely absent from the reasons for failure, particularly when many of the reasons for failure could have been corrected if there had been genuine commitment on the part of top management.

Two other factors emerge from the Collard and Dale research, neither of which are commented on in their paper. First, is the point that the commitment of the board and top management must be 'secured' and an understanding 'sought'. This implies that it is the task of someone already committed to persuade the top people of the value of this tool. While it is impossible for every idea to originate at the top, absolute success can only come with absolute commitment and it would be infinitely better for the concept to start at the top.

Second and by far the more important is their omission of the need for quality circles to be part of a total orientation to both quality and employee involvement. The impression given in the vast majority of studies of quality control circles is that it is an activity outside the normal running of the job. At the extreme this means quality control circles being the 'flavour of the month' management technique, which can be tried for a short time, and if they do not work can be cast aside in favour of another instant remedy. It also results in an attitude developing that 'quality is something we do on the second Tuesday of the month'.

Perhaps better than most the Transport and General Workers Union has understood the connection between Quality Control Circles and the involvement of employees. Indeed its pamphlet on the subject is called *Employee Involvement and Quality Circles – a TGWU guide*.[3] The pamphlet describes Quality Control Circles as 'a management technique which is supposed to harness the expertise of employees in improving all aspects of the quality of products and services. This includes not only product design and manufacture but also delivery, servicing and other features'. Turning to Employee Involvement the pamphlet states that it is 'a similar process of involving groups of employees voluntarily in solving production problems' but then most significantly adds 'It is difficult to distinguish this from other forms of consultative systems such as Quality Circles, Quality of Working Life, Employee Information and Team Briefings. The name 'Employee Involvement' can have a wider interpretation than covering merely quality control.'

The Union clearly understands that the process is really about involving employees and as such it must be central to the everyday running of the business. The TGWU concern is not so much about employees being involved as about the Union *not* being involved. It repeats its adherence to the majority report of the Bullock Committee in 1979 (which advocated the election via the trade unions of employee representatives on Boards of large companies) and states that it is important 'to distinguish between the "Employee Involvement" plans being implemented by some companies and industrial democracy. Certainly where such systems are used to undermine or by-pass union representative structures and collective bargaining they can be positively harmful'. For an organisation which exists to represent its members such an approach is entirely logical but it continues the fundamental fallacy that industrial democracy means the involvement of trade unions whereas it is the involvement of *employees* at their place of work in areas where they can have a meaningful impact that really counts.

Notwithstanding this, in companies with established trade unions it is unrealistic to expect to be able to develop any form of employee involvement in a broad or narrow sense without seeking and obtaining the support of the trade unions. Indeed it would be wrong to do so, for not only would it be an attempt to by-pass legitimately elected representatives, but also an attempt to ignore their wishes. QC circles do fail because of lack of TU support but there is a great difference between open hostility and suspicion. The TGWU, while recognising 'the dangers of so called

Employee Involvement and Quality Circle schemes', does advise members that such schemes

- should not be introduced without union scrutiny and consent
- that representatives should be chosen in line with union representatives machinery
- that where they exist such schemes should be brought in line with union structure and under union control
- and that in no case should they be allowed to undermine union structures or collective bargaining.

Again, while misunderstanding the purpose (e.g. 'representatives') the TGWU does recognise the realities and appears to accept that it will have to live with the concept which does seem to have got beyond the 'flavour of the month'.

The company probably more associated with Quality Control Circles than any other is the Westinghouse Electric Corporation. With some 2000 circles in 200 locations Westinghouse is however moving beyond the 'pure' Quality Control Circle to other forms of participation with the aim of involving everyone – not just the QCC participants – in a broad range of issues relating to the job. Ad hoc teams are being established to handle specific problems and a Field Improvement Programme has been initiated. Under this programme, teams meet on a weekly basis in order to monitor performance and it is claimed that yields have increased by up to 22 per cent by tackling defined problems at these meetings. Other US developments from the QCC theme have been reported by D. Wallace Bell in his *Report on America*.[4] Martin Marietta Aerospace has evolved its Quality Circles into Better Action Teams which no longer concentrate on cost savings for monetary awards. Hewlett Packard is reported as changing Quality Control Circles to Work Centre Groups, for employees were becoming disillusioned with the amount of time they were having to spend preparing presentations rather than on dealing with the issues. 'The Work Centre Groups comprise all the employees in a work group meeting with their supervisor once a week to discuss any problems that may have arisen. They can call in any technical people they may need to help them; and if a problem affects more than one work centre, an ad hoc joint group drawn from all those affected will be set up.'

Regarded as being one of the most successful Quality Circle Companies in the UK, Mullard at Hazel Grove near Manchester sees the practice very much on the lines of the Japanese model. 'A Quality Circle should be aimed at improving the lives of all people.... Circle members strive to create an environment in which women and men can move in the direction of the realisation of human worth and dignity.' The key ingredient for success according to Mullard is the ability to care – about the company, its products and success.

Another company to recognise that Quality Control Circles are not enough is Black & Decker, a non-union company some 20 miles from Nissan's Sunderland plant. Having successfully operated Quality Circles at Spennymore, Co. Durham, since setting up in 1980, the company has in the last year or so been developing a wider approach involving quality, employee involvement and service to the customer. Called Total Customer Service (TCS) it aims

1. To involve all employees (eventually) in the quality improvement and employee involvement process
2. To foster stronger links at shop floor and supervisory level between various work areas and departments and with the companies who supply materials and components to Black & Decker.

Significantly TCS is regarded as compulsory as opposed to the normal voluntary approach to QCC. It takes place in working time with production halted.

The text books are replete with reports on how to set up Quality Control Circles and many consultants make a good living from advising companies on 'How to establish a Quality Circle Programme'. Most companies go through the process of establishing a steering Committee, a facilitator (or co-ordinator), circle leaders, training programmes, problem solving methodology, communication systems, reward policy, evaluation methodology, presentations to management, implementation process, follow up systems, circle extension plans etc.

Deep down, however, when analysing the process we would use in Nissan, we were convinced of three things. First the programme had to be about something more than quality; second that it should be a natural extension of the way a team normally operated and third, we did not want to establish an external bureaucratic structure which might destroy what we hoped would be achieved.

NMUK was, however, also committed to the policy of team working and the development of the individuals within the team. In the words of a paper prepared within NMUK, we therefore felt it 'essential to introduce Quality Circles as a means of improving individual and team development and the participation of staff in the general day to day running of their working areas. The key to success in achieving this development is in ensuring that Quality Circle activity is fully integrated into the job and is not seen as a separate activity'. We therefore regarded QC activity as just one aspect of a programme aimed at achieving employee commitment to continuous improvement in all areas.

However to give substance to the activity and to ensure that we did make progress we thought it sensible also to establish a more formal framework – particularly helpful when considering the larger issues. Thus, in addition to the informal activities, part of the everyday job, we also set up a Steering Committee, very importantly under the Chairmanship of the Director of Production, comprising representatives of all staff to plan the more formal side. Because of the view that problem solving and continuous improvement are part of everyone's job we made the decision not to give any financial reward for achievement – to do so would be to make it special. But recognition of good work is important and thus we left it to the Steering Committee to decide what form this should take. (In the same way Nissan does not have a Suggestions Scheme. Formalising the process makes it something special. When continuous improvement is part of the job you do not need a bureaucratic, time consuming procedure to generate ideas.)

The title chosen for this activity by Nissan is *kaizen* team (building on the general concept of *kaizen* described on page 46). (Interestingly the title was chosen by the British staff, the Japanese feeling more comfortable with Quality Control Circles). While recognising that continuous improvement is part of everyone's job, it is bigger than that, for it does imply the total involvement spoken of by the TGWU. It also reflects the concept of *kaizen* workshops – areas of the plant where manufacturing staff can go to make or improve tooling or fabricate aids to ease the manufacturing process. It recognises that for some issues a formal process to resolve problems may be necessary and that that process will use analytical techniques which will have to be taught. It also means the full involvement of supervisors – in

Nissan they did not need convincing, for having experienced the process in Japan, they needed little encouragement.

Because *kaizen* is part of the team responsibility, it is important that it becomes an integral part of a supervisor's responsibility (in fact not only production supervisors for we determined that this activity would take place in all areas of the Company) and that all supervisors be fully trained in the problem-solving techniques commonly associated with QC activity. The supervisor, the genuine leader of the group, then naturally becomes the leader, at least initially, of problem-solving and continuous improvement activities – although, as experience develops, other team members will be expected to assume leadership of problem-solving groups. Because we regard it as part of everyone's job to strive to improve continuously, the question of whether the activity is voluntary or compulsory does not really arise. We believe that much can be accomplished without setting up a specific structure, particularly with regard to the everyday problems – virtually on the basis of a supervisor or group defining a particular area to be considered and asking a small group to have a go at tackling it.

It is unusual for a Quality Control Circle leader to be the supervisor of the work group on which the circle is based. Some companies, after circles have been established for a time, have found it opportune to move away from this structure. Most notably in the US, Ford agreed with the UAW a specific list of characteristics which hourly paid employee involvement facilitators should possess.

- Strong support for employee involvement philosophy and goals
- Good communication skills
- Self motivating, be a self starter
- Be able to relate effectively with union and management officials at all levels and with lower paid workers
- Have the ability and willingness to learn and apply new skills
- Understand plant operations
- Know plant personnel

One rather feels that someone with such qualifications would be well employed as the Plant Manager! In the UK, Black & Decker, prior to the move to Total Customer Service concept, had 23 of its 34 quality circles led by people other than supervisors.

There is no doubt that this has some attraction and in principle we had nothing against it particularly if a move to a leader other than the Supervisor was for a particular project, and especially if more than one project was being handled. However, the Supervisor *is* the leader of the group. It is his responsiblity in his section to ensure continuous improvement, and to appoint someone else as the formal leader of a *kaizen* team is artificial and to a certain extent diminishes his authority. While it can be argued that good supervisors do not necessarily make good circle leaders, if a supervisor is not a good leader of his section's input then he is *not* a good supervisor. This does not mean that he cannot make specific individuals responsible for specific aspects – indeed he should do this both to spread the word and to help the development of his staff – but the man in charge should *be* the man in charge.

The formal TUC policy expressed in a 1981 statement sees little that is basically new in the idea of Quality Circles and more significantly states 'QC's are a belated recognition of employees' expertise and knowledge and the need to put them to use'. The TUC predictably argues for trade union involvement in the QC process, a sharing of the benefits, a concern about the employment implications of QC and a recognition that the general subject matter of QC must be expanded 'to cover other matters affecting quality and competitiveness such as research and development, marketing and investment'. QC circles are not regarded by the TUC as a substitute for 'more far reaching forms of involvement'.

An alternative view from a Trade Union supporter of quality circles has been put by Eric Hammond, General Secretary of the EETPU. Writing in a DTI booklet on Quality Circles he stated:

> I have no hesitation in advising trade unionists to explore with their management and with their fellow workers how forming such circles can bring benefit to them as individuals as well as to their organisation. Such involvement would improve personal satisfaction and pride in the job as well as boosting our national performance at the level where a real remedy to our problem lies – in the plant and in the company.[5]

The debate between management and most trade unions is therefore often conducted virtually on two separate levels. Management sees the process as one of genuinely involving employees in matters to which they can directly contribute and as such the formal Union structure has no real place *per se*. The wise managers however understand the real world and, when the Unions have an effective voice, recognise the need to involve the Union hierarchy. The Trade Union debate starts off by recognising this point and follows on by insisting on its place – but where? If the circles are small 'the Union' cannot be present at all times but what they can do is discuss (negotiate?) the terms under which the circles are structured and then maintain that the circle is no substitute for real industrial democracy.

There is little doubt that one of the main problems in establishing Quality Control Circles is the attitude of first line supervisors. Collard and Dale's second condition for the successful introduction and operation of Quality Circles is:

> Involve middle management and supervision – it is essential to brief this group and to encourage willing supervisors to participate in and form circles. In addition this group should provide specialist help to circles. Successful involvement of middle management and supervision has been found to strengthen their role and assist their relations with the shop floor by encouraging greater contact and communication.[6]

Again, however, while this remains true, it still treats QC circles as something outside the normal activity of the group.

In summary, quality of work will only be high if the individual is fully motivated. While we may say that quality must be 'built into' the job this will only happen if the right attitude to quality comes from within the individual. No amount of exhortation will achieve genuine commitment to quality – wall posters and slogans will fail. It is a key management responsibility and can be attained only if we realise that it is total motivation that matters – if we cut away the 'quality' leg of the tripod the other two legs will fall also. With genuine commitment to quality comes commitment – and teamworking – in many other aspects of working life.

6 Teamworking and Commitment – Philosophy and Practice

Teamwork and commitment permeate every aspect of the Nissan approach. You cannot have true teamworking and commitment without common terms and conditions of employment, without managers and supervisors who are genuinely interested in keeping people informed and involved, without work practices which encourage flexibility and innovation. To separate certain elements for specific attention under this heading is an almost impossible task.

We have seen in Chapter 2 'Japanese management – separating reality from the myth' that in many respects it is the group or team that is important in Japan. While it is a cliché to say that the group is more important than the individual, the employee who is able to make a very personal contribution but is not a good team player will be regarded as lesser than the individual with a lower personal contribution but a higher commitment to the common cause.

While again emphasising that we are talking of trends rather than absolutes, western society is much more oriented towards the individual. As with the Japanese there are many theories as to the reasons for this – in the United States it is the 'frontier' thesis, the growth of the nation dependent on individual hunters continually pushing forward the boundaries. In Europe, the growth of the Protestant ethic and its influence on the pursuit of individual wealth, as put forward by Max Weber,[1] was in fact the contrasting starting point of Morishima's *Why has Japan Succeeded*. Whatever the reasons, the fact is that the Japanese worker expects to belong to a team in all aspects of his life; the westerner often chooses not to belong – and certainly not to any team associated with his work.

What however do we mean by teamworking in a western environment? In Continental the key paragraph of the Company's philosophy statement read 'What we are seeking is the total involvement of all employees with their jobs so that while

75

management has the ultimate responsibility for planning, directing and control, this responsibility does not need to be exercised in an autocratic matter (nor must it be abdicated). We are aiming to establish a team approach in which self-control and self-direction results in individuals regulating their own performance in harmony with the objectives of the Company'.

Specific reference in the Nissan philosophy statement is much simpler. 'We recognise that all staff have a valued contribution to make as individuals but in addition believe that this contribution can be most effective within a teamworking environment. . . . Our aim is to build a Company with which people can identify and to which they feel commitment'. In simple terms therefore teamworking means having all employees committed to the aims and objectives of the Company, ie. recognising that each individual has a valued contribution to make but that we should aim for everyone working in the same direction. This is reflected in the Nissan–AEU agreement which includes in its General Principles the need

to promote mutual trust and co-operation between the Company, its employees and the Union
to recognise that all employees, at whatever level, have a valued part to play in the success of the Company
to seek actively the contributions of all employees in furtherance of these goals.

Other companies aiming for this concept of teamworking have expressed it differently.

Hitachi, in its policy document *A New Future at Hirwaun* which was put forward following its takeover from GEC, set out three guiding principles 'which underlie the Hitachi management philosophy – sincerity, pioneering spirit and harmony.' The principles are expressed in very Japanese terms and it is unlikely that a western company would use these specific words. It then goes on to state that 'The principles are exemplified by co-operation. Inside the Company the assertion of different opinions is encouraged. However, once a conclusion is reached, all company members are expected to co-operate to achieve the objectives'. Again this very much reflects the Japanese philosophy of full discussion prior to a decision followed by commitment to that decision.

Perhaps the most celebrated Company philosophy belongs to IBM. In its booklet *Employment with IBM – Principles at Work* the company's respect for the individual is emphasised. It recognises the individual nature of each employee's contribution and that 'concern for the individual cements the foundation of our personnel philosophy in full employment, promotion from within, equal opportunity, pay for performance and single status'. Most importantly IBM also recognises that 'no employee relations system is infallible. With a human element, mistakes will happen. Our challenge is to keep our practice in line with our principle'. When asked, after employees had rejected trade union recognition, what were the reasons for IBM's success, Len Peach, then IBM Director of Personnel, said 'Start with a green field, introduce the policies and practices we have, work at it and in about 25 years you should produce a similar result'.

In further defining respect for the individual, IBM underlines some common factors – 'Drawing out the best of individuals' energies, talents, skills, creativity and adaptability, rewarding individuals for their achievements and contribution, creating opportunities for individuals to develop, ensuring that the individual's voice can be heard, protecting the rights and dignity of the individual and providing a basic sense of security for the individual'. It is against this background however that IBM seeks commitment and involvement of all its people – 'just as the company has obligations to the individual so employees have obligations to IBM'. and 'To help implement these basic principles effectively and to help develop "team spirit" IBM has consistently encouraged a close employee–manager relationship. Within that, the manager is responsible for effective leadership, good employee relations and direct two-way communications.'

Eaton Ltd, an American company which has made significant changes to the management style of its UK companies, has published its own philosophy statement. Comprising a number of key principles, the statement is prefaced 'Eaton understands that the success of the company depends, ultimately, on the performance of its employees. Sustained, high performance is most likely when there is a high level of individual commitment to the goals of their organisation. This Eaton Philosophy strives for such commitment by recognising the potential for positive contributions from all employees, and by committing the organisation to work towards the development of an atmosphere in which these contributions can, and will, be made'. Eaton's principles emphasise 'Mutual trust, mutual respect, and the individual freedom necessary for exceptionally high employee performance'. Its key points are:

- Focus on the positive behaviour of employees
- Encourage employee involvement in decisions
- Communicate with employees in a timely and candid way, with emphasis on face-to-face communications
- Compensate employees competitively under systems which reward excellence
- Provide training for organisational/individual success
- Maintain effective performance appraisal systems
- Emphasise promotion from within throughout the company
- Select managers and supervisors who demonstrate an appropriate blend of human relations skills and technical competence.

In citing an example of the principles in practice Alan Best, Eaton's European Director of Operations, has shown that by setting up small groups of operators and supervisors and asking them to redesign plant layouts, inventories have been more than halved and lead time is measured in days rather than weeks. However, says Best 'the improvement in employee involvement is greater still because in a working environment such as this, employees really do feel that they have a significant role to play in the management of the company'.[2]

In the year that it was granted its Royal Charter (1985) the Industrial Society introduced a new element into its campaigning; a 'Charter for People at Work' – a six-paragraph statement encapsulating the Society's principles. As an organisation which is representative of all sectors of industry, public service and commerce, and speaks for both management and some trade unions, the Society's views are well respected. The Charter states: 'As leaders and representatives from every level of industry, commerce, the public service and the trade union movement, we believe the future prosperity of this country can only be ensured by the fullest involvement of all people in their work. We recognise that the future is the responsibility of every one of us. We believe that:

- The greatest challenge is cooperating with change – both technological and structural. All change must be supported by effective leadership from those accountable for involving people at every level.

— Views of people at work should be consistently sought and taken into account by management.

— To gain flexibility, commitment and the highest level of customer satisfaction and a sense of achievement we need to explain decisions and relevant business issues at regular intervals.

— We should take the lead in providing opportunities for individuals to contribute in the most appropriate way. Industry and commerce must in turn contribute to the community if it is to provide employment, resources and hope for the future.

— Individuals should be encouraged to participate fully in the activities of their trade union. Productive management–union relations should include the positive commitment from both parties to the aims and success of the enterprise and to the achievement of justice for the people involved.

— We should work to ensure that the whole community, especially the young, understand why the creation of wealth matters, both for future employment and for society as a whole.

If such philosophical statements are to be true to themselves then they should be developed by the team. While there has to be the originating individual spark, that spark can best flourish in a team atmosphere. In both Continental and Nissan the development of the team philosophy was a practical demonstration of that philosophy at work. We needed a coherent written statement on how the companies were to be run, to which we could return when the going got tough. We recognised that whatever the philosophy turned out to be, we would not always be able to maintain it one hundred per cent – particularly when production demands were at their most stringent. However, we felt that if we were able to write something down we would determine that point to which to return when blown off course. Failing this, the companies would be blown by whichever wind was strongest at the time and once off course it is difficult to return if there is no known starting point. Thus in both cases, all managers sat together to develop the statement with a starting point inspired by words used in Shell (UK) in a similar situation at Teesport a few years previously. We were attempting to remove the traditional barriers and achieve 'a fundamental change in attitude on the part of employees to a point where in a climate of mutual trust and confidence it becomes possible for all employees to commit themselves fully to the Company's objective of having its work carried out with maximum efficiency and productivity'.

In concluding these statements aimed at building teams it was interesting how closely the ideas of practising managers came to those of the early behavioural scientists – the Herzbergs, Maslows and McGregor's of this world. While in recent years academics have attempted to demolish many of the early theories it was instructive to find that the thoughts of managers working every day on the shop floor, are not a million miles away from the early theories, now much criticised because they are 'improvable'. The Continental managers themselves concluded that immediate tangible benefits – money, working conditions etc. do not necessarily motivate people or assist in achieving commitment but if they are not right you get problems. The management task is to achieve commitment through motivation and this you get by recognising the value of individuals, their contribution etc.

In Continental we recognised that management often has to take the initiative but that in so doing it is vital to encourage creativity on the part of all employees and in arriving at decisions, resolving problems or establishing objectives we should involve people who have the ability to contribute. This need not be within formal procedures. Real involvement is most effectively achieved by establishing good informal relationships where regular consultation and discussion happens as a matter of course. We are talking about involving *all* employees, not, as is often the case, restricting such involvement to representatives of employees.

By the time we came to discuss such issues at Nissan the criticisms of the early behavioural theorists had become even more severe. Thus while to the practising manager there remained a conviction that there is some sort of 'needs hierarchy' and some support for the ideas of intrinsic and extrinsic job factors contributing separately to job satisfaction, there remains little academic consensus that the two sets of factors affect behaviour in the way hypothesised by Herzberg. Nevertheless we did discuss some of the more up to date thinking, culled mainly from Robertson and Smith's *Motivation and Job Design*.[3]

Bearing in mind the objective of teamworking and commitment the summary in Robertson and Smith is of considerable practical value. Building on the work of the later behavioural theorists they have listed a number of factors important in developing commitment and which Nissan management found to be of considerable value.

- Employees should understand the link between effort and performance.
- Employees should have the competence and confidence to translate effort into performance.
- Control systems should be introduced only when necessary.
- Performance requirements should be expressed in terms of hard but attainable goals.
- Employees should participate in setting these goals, feedback should be regular, informative and easy to interpret.
- Employees should be praised for good performance.
- Rewards should be seen to be equitable.
- Rewards should be tailored to individual requirements and preference.
- Employees' psychological and physical well-being should be seen as important.
- Jobs should be designed to maximise skill variety, task identity, task significance, autonomy, feedback and provide opportunities for learning and growth.
- Organisation and job changes should be brought about through consultation and discussion.

One UK company which has made conscious efforts to develop teamworking is Carreras Rothman in Spennymoor, County Durham. Indeed a comment made after a Nissan visit was that we could save a lot of money by sending our people twenty miles down the road to C-R rather than travelling thousands of miles to Japan! C-R call their exercise Group Working, and the C-R objectives very specifically aim for a high level of commitment. Indeed the four managers designated to set up the factory first went through their own team building course.

Included in the C-R package of measures are the Company uniform, single status canteen, common car parking and minimal job descriptions. But importantly C-R has paid considerable attention to the layout of the plant (and their rest room concept directly influenced Nissan's approach) and in particular they developed their own version of the Volvo 'little factory within a factory' in what have become 'task units'. Under the leadership of group leaders, the groups have their own budgets, collect their own data, determine their own methods of communication, do their own housekeeping and meet to discuss production plans and ways of improving work methods. A Work Research Unit paper resulting from a study of Carreras-Rothman quoted an employee on the value of group meetings 'they keep us well informed production-wise – whether sales are going up or down, whether they are opening new markets'. A group leader said 'You don't need a big stick with people. I treat people as adults'.[4]

Building on academic work, combining it with practical experience and learning from our Japanese colleagues and training, Nissan managers developed a philosophy statement aimed at building an effective company in which all are working towards the same aims and objective. Within the overall framework of wishing 'to achieve mutual trust and cooperation between all people within the company', the philosophy statement includes:

> We will develop and expand the contribution of all staff by strongly emphasising training and the expansion of everyone's capabilities.

> We seek to delegate and involve staff in discussion and decision-making, particularly in those areas in which they can effectively contribute so that all may participate in the efficient running of NMUK.

> Within the bounds of commercial confidentiality we would like everyone to know what is happening in our company, how we are performing and what we plan.

> We want information and views to flow freely upward, downward and across our company.

This statement was signed by the Managing Director, printed and issued to all employees. It represents the point to which we aim to return when blown off course.

The development of teamworking and commitment philosophies has not unnaturally attracted the attention of the academics. Writing in the *Harvard Business Review*, Professor Richard E. Walton[5] contrasts the 'commitment' approach to the early management theories emphasising 'control'. Quoting from American experience, Professor Walton establishes a commitment-based model where 'jobs are designed to be broader than before, to combine planning and implementation and to include efforts to upgrade operations, not just maintain them. Individual responsibilities are expected to change as conditions change, and often teams, not individuals, are the organisational units accountable for performance. With management hierarchies relatively flat and differences in status minimised, control and lateral co-ordination depend on shared goals and expertise rather than formal position-determined influence.' Under this strategy 'performance expectations are high and serve not to define minimum standards but to provide "stretch objectives", emphasise continuous improvement and reflect the requirements of the market place'.

Significantly among the Companies quoted by Professor Walton are two from the US motor industry where the term Employee Involvement (with initial capitals) has been much used. Much work has been done in General Motors where, after much initial wrangling with the UAW Local 235, the Gear and Axle Plant developed Employee Participation Circles aimed at improving communications, developing a sense of ownership and creating a problem-solving attitude. After four years of development a Union official indicated that advances had been substantial, 'Communication has improved dramatically on three fronts – within each plant, among the eight plants and between the plants and outside vendors. The employee participation program has also led to an open discussion of problems – both those that cause individual workers a hardship on the job and those that jeopardize the quality of the production'.[6]

It was the General Motors Quality of Working Life programme which takes different forms in different plants that directly influenced Ford US and, subsequently, Ford of Britain. By the early 1980s Ford's surveys showed that quality was a major factor determining customer purchasing decisions and there came a realisation that 'making quality a central issue was unlikely to succeed with the "adversarial union – management tradition"'[7] The Ford term was 'Employee Involvement' which Ford US and the UAW agreed 'held the promise to create a more satisfying and stimulating work environment'. Ford's aim was to improve job satisfaction but also to reduce absenteeism, labour turnover and product defects – a recognition of the interlinking and mutual dependency of these factors.

In Ford US the UAW and the Company worked together and the programme has been successful. In mid-1982 the Ford National Joint Committee on Employee Involvement conducted a survey of those locations which had an established EI programme and found that 83 per cent thought they had the opportunity to work with others in solving employee-related problems compared with 33 per cent before the programme. Awareness of costs improved from 46 per cent to 80 per cent and employee satisfaction from 58 to 82 per cent. 91 per cent thought their Union was right to support EI programmes. One of the conclusions of the study was 'Employees believe EI is having a beneficial effect on their jobs and work environment and the EI process is working well where there is a high level of local management and local union commitment. Comparing the present to the pre-EI perceptions the EI participants registered an average 30 percentage point increase in favourable responses to all survey questions'.

Unfortunately the Ford US success has not been repeated in Britain. The trade unions had a significant role in frustrating earlier attempts to introduce Quality Control Circles due to their dislike of anything which could be seen as management talking directly to workers. Similarly, attempts to introduce Employee Involvement foundered. Initially accepted by the staff unions EI virtually became an item on the bargaining table and acceptance was withdrawn when no agreement could be reached on discussions over headcount figures. With the manual unions it has never left the starting line.

This trade union hostility is echoed elsewhere in the UK. The left wing Labour Research Department[8] reports shop stewards as being opposed to British Airways 'customer first teams' in the belief that they reduce members commitment to the union. At May and Baker the TGWU withdrew from the QWL programme during pay and conditions negotiations. Perhaps it is unrealistic to attempt to divorce employee involvement from the daily cut and thrust and maybe it can only work where there is already a high degree of trust. Just as Quality Control Circles cannot by themselves bring about an improvement in quality, then employee involvement programmes in the UK cannot by themselves develop commitment.

And this is the problem. We spend vast amounts of time talking and negotiating about employee involvement and very little time actually involving employees. As with so many of these ideas – the 'flavours of the month' that will be our managerial salvation – we construct an edifice which simply invites opposition. At its basic level, involving employees is simply about a foreman saying to his people 'what do you think about...?' It needs no special meetings – it can be done as he passes by. What it *does* need is the will to make it happen – and that is what we so often lack.

What then does a Company have to do to build an atmosphere of teamworking and commitment? First of all what it does *not* do is to send people on team-building courses, although in some cases these may act as a catalyst. There is no limit to the number of such programmes, and Training Departments are inundated with literature from organisations purporting to put people through expensive itineraries which will return them convinced that by working as a team they will achieve more than by acting individually.

In Nissan if there is one aspect to be singled out as important in team building and commitment it is the five minute meeting at the start of the day. This is something we have learned directly from Japan, it is successful in Nissan's plant in Smyrna, Tennessee and its importance in NMUK cannot be overestimated. In Japan, employees are prepared for work at their place of work at the start of the working day. But the place of work is not their position on the production line; it is at their meeting place, usually the rest area. It is here, in Japan, that the famous exercise period takes place – usually two minutes. To anyone who has pushed his or her way through the Tokyo rush hour (which makes Oxford Street seem like a stroll down a country lane) or is about to start an eight hour shift on the production line, this exercise period can add little, physically, to the well-being of the individual. However, to the Japanese foreman the important point is that his team is doing something together. Even more important however is the fact that the exercise period is followed by a further few minutes in which the team talks together. Every day the foreman talks *with* his people.

This talk is frequently about quality but it will also be used to discuss schedule changes, work redistribution, process changes, training, the introduction of a new member or social events. Sometimes, team members other than the foreman will cover certain points. Most of the discussion is about matters that directly affect the team in their daily work and will originate from the supervisor himself or may be based on discussions and meetings he has had with his manager. Only occasionally is there a 'great message from on high'. The philosophy is that if something is worth telling it should be told immediately and the best method of communication is face to face. It is far more important to establish fast communication on most matters and risk having slightly different versions going out than it is to slow down the communication route by waiting for the 100 per cent accurate report to come, typed, from a central office. Of course there will be times when accuracy is critical but the number of occasions when this is of paramount importance are limited. And it is important that everyone should be involved. This is not just a shop floor activity, it is a company wide activity. It is important that the receptionist, who is often the first contact point for a visitor, knows what quality levels are being achieved or what has been discussed at the weekly Executive meeting and it is the job of her manager to ensure that she does. If this is not done how can she feel herself part of the team?

Contrast this with the normal British approach where at the start of shift the poor foreman has so much to do that he has little time to talk to his workers – and if he does it is to castigate them for lateness or failing to meet yesterday's schedule. In an attempt to improve matters the Industrial Society has been at the forefront in persuading managements to actually hold meetings with employees and has developed the concept of Briefing Groups. The theory is that such groups meet on a regular basis, say monthly, that messages are formulated at the top or can be interspersed at various levels and at an agreed time production is halted for the messages to be conveyed. It is emphasised that this should be a two way process so that employees are also able to raise items and comment on the information received.

Under the Industrial Society system, Co-ordinators are appointed and the Co-ordinator check list for introducing Team Briefing consists of no fewer than 13 steps – including presentations to the Board, the union, drawing up structure charts, organising paperwork, running courses etc. Once the system is in operation the detailed process lists ten steps, the first of which is 'Throughout the month all briefers collect snippets of information and facts on team progress in their briefing folders'. Then 'The briefers' managers will check the local input... and comment if necessary'. Specific time should be set aside at board or executive meetings to determine what information should be passed down the line.

In practice Briefing Groups have rarely succeeded in this form over long periods. Stopping production seems acceptable for the first few occasions but top management commitment does wane when immediate results are not obvious. But it also becomes increasingly difficult for senior management to think of meaningful messages to pass down the line and what starts off as a pleasure becomes a chore which is passed to the Personnel Manager 'to think up what to say next week'. The theory is fine and the purpose that people should talk to each other absolutely right but making a big event out of what should be a normal everyday occurrence must mitigate against continuing success. Within the motor manufacturing industry the only company which appears to have had any success with the more traditional type of briefing group (once a month for 15–30 minutes with messages being passed down the line) is Jaguar Cars. But then with Jaguar such sessions are only part of a thought-out total concept. They are not a 'stand alone' panacea superimposed on an established system in which nothing else changes.

Equally, the sacred cows of modern industrial life, the company newspaper and more lately the corporate video, have little role to play in *real* communication and teambuilding. By definition they take time to produce but, as stated, if anything is worth telling it should be told quickly and normally it should be the immediate supervisor who does the telling. Not only does this give immediacy but also develops his role as the genuine leader of the group. He who communicates is king!

In Nissan the morning discussion takes place in the team's meeting area. It is typical in British industry to have what virtually amounts to a 'no go' area – where foremen fear to tread. In other companies there is no such rest area at all. Whichever way round, it is rare for the foreman to be able to socialise with his workers. Often relief breaks will be on a staggered basis so that, whatever the facilities, the group as a whole can never get together. The Nissan solution has been to construct large meeting areas (about 20 feet by 15 feet), one for each supervisor and his team. These are spacious, well-lit places where the supervisor has his desk, where there are lockers, tables and benches, blackboards, notice boards, recreational facilities and most importantly a boiler to make tea and coffee. In some the team has brought in a refrigerator, there are often photographs of the team members, others have comprehensive notice boards covering everything from press cuttings to spaces for team members to write up ideas for improving the job. Block relief is taken with, often, someone stopping a few minutes early to make the tea, thus on several occasions each day the supervisor and his team are able to be together as a group. It is in these areas that reports are prepared, *kaizen* discussions take place, process sheets rewritten, etc. It is difficult to underestimate the importance of these areas.

Essential to this process is an acceptance on the part of managers and supervisors that they have no monopoly of wisdom on the best way of performing a task or on making improvements. So often in British industry we regard it as a criticism of our performance if a subordinate is able to come up with a better idea. We believe that we should have thought of it and regard such suggestions as a challenge to our authority. Nothing could be more wrong. Managers and supervisors should have as a prime objective the bringing out of new ideas and concepts from their staff. Their task is to create the environment in which new thinking is encouraged and welcomed. If a subordinate is able to develop an improvement the boss is to be congratulated not criticised. Only in that way can we create the environment in which genuine involvement takes place.

Just as the team will break together so will the company eat together. Single dining facilities are regarded as one of the most overt manifestations of single status and these are rapidly becoming the norm in British industry. The Industrial Society's 1986 *Survey of Catering Prices, Costs and Subsidies*[9] covering about 480 catering operations found that about 60 per cent of the companies taking part operated single status dining rooms compared to 40 per cent in 1980. Perhaps more than anything else such a facility demonstrates a company's determination to do things differently, although if the change is brought about by economics rather than principle – and little else changes – then single dining rooms will by themselves do little to change attitudes.

To managers, used to the privilege of separate and better dining facilities, the change may at first be difficult to accept but very quickly they become proud of it and enjoy taking – often very senior – visitors into the dining room and making them queue up with everyone else. Change is often opposed on the basis that confidential discussions need to take place over lunch, in private. But no-one else has ever been prevented from having a private discussion over lunch if he wishes. The other side of the coin is the view that single dining rooms allow people to mix. Theoretically this may be true but in practice people are creatures of habit – they tend to sit with those they know, generally from the same department or peers from another section. Lunchtime is a time to relax and this is difficult if a senior manager from one department is seeking to have a somewhat artificial conversation with a junior employee he does not know. The value of single status dining rooms does not come from actual mixing but from the fact that the Company does not erect barriers preventing mixing. The fact that everyone joins the same queue and eats the same food (which apart from anything else ensures that quality is maintained) does develop the attitude of 'all being in it together'.

The same argument can be used for car parking. Most companies in the UK (and in Japan) have reserved car parking spaces for senior executives – often close to the door. Many companies are now abolishing this privilege and car parking is on a 'first come first served' basis. The fact that the Managing Director has to walk just as far – in the rain – from his parking space to the front door is regarded by many as being important in developing teamworking. The ability to lead does not depend on privilege but on capability in the job and those who believe that they have to retain the outward manifestations of rank to gain respect are deluding only themselves. In fact attempts to maintain these privileges are regarded as a demonstration that executives do not really mean what they say. In such an environment actions are regarded as speaking louder than words and calls for teamwork by executives who maintain privilege are more likely to be disregarded than if the executives demonstrate *their* real commitment by living at the same level as others.

As, if not more, important is the actual work environment. Office staff are generally accustomed to clean, well lit areas. British factories are invariably decorated in delicate shades of sludge green! Components are piled floor to ceiling and the field of vision is frequently restricted to no more than a few feet. There is no reason why manual workers, within obvious constraints of the job, should not have working conditions equivalent to those of office staff. This means clean, brightly coloured areas. The Nissan plant is full of blues, oranges, reds, yellows etc. It is maintained in a clean condition by the people who work in it and when walking in the factory you feel a sense of guilt if you want to throw a piece of paper anywhere other than in the proper receptacles. People working in such an environment take a pride in their place of work and are pleased to show visitors around. It certainly helps car sales!

Once starting down this route there is no logical stopping place – open plan offices, desks, furniture, uniforms – each company has to make its own decisions. Even the most egalitarian executive would be loth to give up his company car although in the UK this is now such a well-established part of the executive employment package that loss of this privilege is regarded as a non-starter. Anyway, along with the higher salary it is something for others to aim for!

Many managers claim they have an open-door policy but few really do. Appointments have to be made or, if not, a secretary has to be passed. The door may not actually be open, but if it is the visitor still has to go through the open door – and this itself is a psychological barrier. Much better to have a 'no door' policy in which people are free to wander up, to hover if you are talking or to call across the room. While initially disconcerting, the fact that there is no physical barrier to anyone is in itself very important – and then if people are encouraged to use the facility the inconvenience to the manager is far outweighed by the benefit to the staff. And that is what is important – no barriers, being accessible and being willing to talk to anyone at almost any time.

'Look at the rubbish they've sent me this week. How do they expect me to do my job with this lot?' A not uncommon cry emerges from British industry at the start of shift on a Monday morning when new starters meet their foreman for the first time. While the foreman's initial assessment may not always be accurate it remains a fact that the arrival on the shop floor of a batch of new starters will often be the first meeting between the new employee and his immediate boss. Because he has had no involvement in their selection the foreman has no real commitment to his new employees but equally it means that the employee has no personal commitment to his foreman. If there are problems it is easier to blame them on someone else and do little to resolve them than it is to bring about an improvement.

It was as a result of this situation that both Continental and Nissan decided to directly involve the Supervisors in the selection of the people who would work for them. The Supervisor is involved throughout the selection process and is the person who makes the final decision. Not only that, it is the Supervisor who phones the successful applicant to offer the job and who then meets the applicant to talk through the job and *his* expectations of the new employee. This has two significant effects: it makes the Supervisor committed to his staff – if there are problems he has only himself to blame and will work harder to rectify the situation. Second, it starts the bond between the employee and the Supervisor – at the very least he respects the Supervisor's judgement. There can be no better way of starting the teambuilding process.

One of the oldest and now least-discussed activities which may help teamworking in a Company is sport. Long regarded as a chore by the 'progressive' personal specialist – Sports and Social Clubs are often thought of as old fashioned. Loved by the Chairman when asked to present prizes and by the few regular participants, the vast majority of employees ignore them except perhaps for the Christmas party. Many companies have sold off under-utilised facilities – usually to cries of anguish but to no long-term detriment to the company and its relationships with its employees.

Where teamworking and commitment do not exist in a company no amount of sports and social activities will create it. However, where the commitment is already there and, most importantly, where the desire emerges from the staff rather than being imposed from above – such activities can reinforce that commitment. Japanese and American companies do this much better than the British. In NMUK we did not try to force the pace, but gradually five-a-side football, badminton, athletics, table tennis and even parachute jumping (organised by one of the receptionists) have emerged. At the first five-a-side competition half the company was involved and this has led to spontaneous matches between numerous departments. Badminton courts have been marked out between the production lines in the plant, fishing trips organised, people asked to wear Nissan tee shirts in the Great North Run. Once such activity develops – because people want to socialise with others within the company – then the company can, unobtrusively, help. And this extends to social activities as well as sport.

Without doubt one of the most celebrated – and most misinterpreted exercises in teambuilding has taken place at Volvo's Kalmar plant where production began in 1974. Many still believe that Volvo's contribution was to employ groups of people in building the whole car – or, at least, significant proportions of it. Formally designated 'dock assembly' this process entailed the partially-completed vehicle being automatically guided into a 'dock' assembly area with work then being undertaken on a stationary vehicle by two or three operators. Dock assembly at Volvo, Kalmar has been abolished! Because of the increase in the number of model variants it became increasingly difficult to store components and they found that failures to complete tasks on time caused considerable difficulties to the production flow. The official report on Volvo[10] also stated 'The workers say that they do not regret the disappearance of the dock assembly, which was sometimes experienced as stressful. To be sure dock assembly gave more freedom to some workers, but at the same time there was always some uncertainty as to exactly where they were in the work cycle at any particular moment and how much time remained for the allotted tasks'.

The success of Volvo comes therefore not from its method of assembly. Teamworking and commitment have little to do with the actual method of organising work. While group working, as it is sometimes called, may require people to work together, there is no reason why this should lead to teamworking and commitment in the sense described in this chapter – indeed it is possible to envisage the opposite occurring. The nature of teamworking in our sense can be developed among people working individually just as, if not more, easily among those working together. It depends on what you call the team.

The basic building block at Volvo, Kalmar, is the assembly team – what they call the 'little factory within the factory'. Within these teams work is organised in a variety of ways – individual tasks, two-man teams working along the line on a variety of tasks etc. Work may be distributed within the team by the team, and the team takes charge of breaking in new members. 'The cohesiveness in the team is so strong that pool workers, who are temporarily assigned to a different team, usually come back to their home team areas for coffee breaks'. Within each foreman's team there have been established results groups which receive considerable amounts of information about performance and financial achievements. The results group has 'its own precisely limited production tasks, its own personnel including specialists and union representatives, its own leisure areas and its own financial framework'. Quality is required to be built in – not inspected in – and in the results-linked payment system the quality index is a large component of the wage calculation.

Volvo staff have a very positive view about the team approach. In a survey of 67 workers, 23 thought team working was 'good', 31 'rather good', four 'rather poor' and to nine it was 'not applicable'. The fact however that nine thought it 'not applicable' is as significant as the 54 rating it 'good' or 'rather good'. It suggests that the employees and the surveyor still believe that teamworking is about working in groups. It is not! Perhaps this accounts for some of the less favourable Volvo statistics. Five or six years after the start of production labour turnover was up to 20 to 25 per cent (by 1983 by using the 'godfather' system – helping and supporting new employees – this was down to 5 per cent). Sickness absenteeism is about 10 per cent – not figures which suggest high commitment levels.

It is interesting to note, however, that in its latest plant, Uddevalla, Volvo has returned to its concept of teams of around 20 people being responsible for building complete sections of the car and aims to abolish the assembly line altogether. Under this batch work system each operator could have a job cycle of up to two hours, it being Volvo's view that if individual job cycles exceed ten minutes it is necessary to make the very significant jump to a totally different method of production. The original Kalmar dock assembly process was halted partly because of material supply problems and partly because of difficulties within the group of people. Clearly Volvo believes that it has solved the material supply problems and it remains to be seen if employee reaction is as planned.

The Volvo view of a little factory within a factory echoed across the Atlantic. The General Motor plant in Freemont, California, suffered from all the typical problems of the motor industry – low productivity, poor quality, strikes, etc. GM closed the plant, and for two years its employees were on lay-off. In 1983 GM entered into a joint venture with Toyota to reopen the plant. A new subsidiary was established – NUMMI (New United Motors Manufacturing Incorporated) – a deal was signed with the UAW, and about 90 per cent of the new workers were the old ones rehired. Today NUMMI has among the highest quality in GM; attitudes and efficiency have totally changed and Freemont is a success story.

What has changed? Not the labour or the union. Although a four press line stamping plant was added and body construction totally renovated, the most significant difference is that the management group is new and has brought with it a new approach, at the heart of which is emphasis on the team. But also they aim for mutual trust and respect, empower people to solve problems and continuously improve, encourage personal responsibility and goal setting, lead by example, let those affected by a decision have a say in it and recognise good performance. All this is within the 'hard' objectives of profit, quality, cost and schedule.

Within NUMMI the *production* team is regarded as the centre and all other teams have a prime task of supporting the production team. Their approach is that 'no need of the production team member should be unfulfilled' and to understand these needs all people have to work on the production line for a period. So often in industry the indirect service departments regard themselves as more important than production. Very consciously NUMMI has turned the tables. It was NUMMI that developed the concept of the *kaizen* workshop (subsequently adopted by NMUK) whereby shop floor personnel can go to work on modifications they believe will help them in the job.

NUMMI's selection process emphasises the 'soft' skills. Does the candidate fit in with the team? Once appointed, a team member is expected to remain with his team for a considerable time but if an individual requests a move the receiving team will meet the 'candidate' to see if the fit is right. They also find that workers, when trusted, respected and given responsibility, respond accordingly. The managers lead by example. It is no good a manager expecting his supervisors to consult and communicate with their staff if the manager does not consult and communicate with the supervisors. To fail in this is rather like instruction once given to the author '*Tell* them we're going to consult!'

There is little doubt that there are many companies throughout the western industrialised world which are moving towards teamworking and commitment even though there is no universal definition of its meaning – nor should there be. Said Professor Walton 'In 1970 only a few plants in the United States were systematically revising their approach to the workforce. By 1975 hundreds of plants were involved. Today I estimate that at least a thousand plants are in the process of making a comprehensive change and that many times that number are somewhere in the transitional stage'.[11] In the UK we are some way behind but we will get there.

In conclusion, teamworking and commitment are difficult to define but you know it when you see it; or perhaps more accurately, feel it. Teamworking is not dependent on people working in groups but upon everyone working towards the same aims and objectives. It cannot be achieved by introducing a 'flavour of the month' technique, be it a return to 'old fashioned' sporting activities or by sending people on the latest consultant-inspired course. It is something which develops because management genuinely believes in it and acts accordingly – and recruits or promotes people who have this same belief. Put very simply, 'If you do not genuinely believe in it, don't try it or you will end up worse than before'.

7 Commitment – Not Sickness – Determines Attendance

In Chapter 1 we have seen that for many reasons the manual worker has for generations been treated by employers as a second-class citizen – a factor of production not to be trusted. In progressing from 'Them and Us' to just 'Us', the area that causes most concern to managements is whether or not manual workers will abuse the 'privilege' of being accorded the same arrangements as white-collar workers on lateness, attendance and sickness benefit.

Traditionally, the manual worker is paid by the hour and frequently is not paid for time lost due to lateness or absence – indeed many companies have erected elaborate systems to ensure that not only is payment stopped but also a disciplinary procedure invoked. In contrast, the white-collar salaried employee has been trusted to be at work on time and, certainly in recent years, has rarely been disciplined or stopped pay when late or absent.

This attitude prevails today, and accordingly most companies place considerable weight on the accurate measurement and documentation of manual workers' timekeeping and attendance. The widespread practice of clocking, (used by nearly 90 per cent of manual workers in the UK), enables companies not only to have an accurate basis for timekeeping, and the subsequent deduction of pay, but also a record for use in disciplinary procedures. It is also argued that time recording allows accurate measurement of overtime worked and provides a good indication of who is on site at any time. These latter arguments while undoubtedly true are equally so for the white-collar workers who do not clock.

'Clocking in' is regarded by many manual workers as being demeaning and is disliked particularly when they see it as part of the process by which they are stopped pay for lateness. Practices on this vary. Some companies stop pay on a minute for minute basis, others allow a period of grace on a daily or weekly basis (sometimes developing into the 'lateness allowance') and some have the policy of not allowing people to start work for, say fifteen minutes, if they are but two or three minutes late. Clocking can in fact generate a high degree of antagonism out of all proportion to its value, and many managers will be able to cite examples of abuse and sabotage of the clocks. One favourite method has been to pour syrup or paint into the mechanism! In other companies, particularly where 'job and finish' operates, the practice of clocking other people in and out is prevalent. In some companies it became necessary for foremen to stand over the clocks, or for mobile clocks to be introduced, which were wheeled out at start and finish time and then locked away.

To a certain extent the abuses described above are regarded as a game by manual workers. Perhaps a more serious effect of the practice of stopping pay for lateness is the attitude that it develops. The clock has become the mechanism for lateness control and stoppage of pay and it has frequently been argued by shop stewards that if an employee is automatically stopped pay for being late, that is the penalty, and he should not suffer additionally under the company's disciplinary code. For some employees the fact that they will lose pay if late is an incentive to get to work on time; for others the attitude develops that 'If I'm late I will lose pay, the company lose my work, so that is a fair trade'. Thus the employee may not bother to hurry for work if he feels he can afford the loss.

Equally serious is the attitude, which many companies have allowed to develop over the years, that clocking-in time is starting time. Many companies have their clocks sited at the main gate or at central points within the factory. Thus an eight o'clock start can mean clocking on at eight, then walking to the locker room, changing and then walking to the work area. Even for those who are on time this process can mean that real work does not actually begin until well after the official start time. The reverse situation takes place at the end of shift where the queue to clock out dead on the dot is the normal pattern in many companies with actual work having finished many minutes before. These practices are particularly prevalent in line production industries, where the management call for 'bell to bell' working has gone largely unheeded. Thus, the production workers may arrive at the actual work area at various times after the formal start time, and the poor foreman will be trying to determine if he has a full crew while actually working on the line to avoid too many jobs being missed. At the end of the shift, employees will work ahead to make that extra time with, inevitably, adverse effects on quality.

A result of the traditional attitude to manual workers' time-keeping is the so called 'lateness control procedure', whereby the company determines a system, which requires an employee to proceed through the disciplinary procedure at a rate dependent on how many times he is late over a specified period. Typically, such a procedure might allow for three latenesses in a month before an oral recorded warning is given; the next three latenesses may result in a first written warning; then a second written warning, one day suspension, three days suspension and finally, after many months, dismissal. Of course, the trade union then negotiates an allowance for 'good time keeping', which provides for the employee to revert to a previous stage in the event of his falling below the stipulated level in any month. The company then seeks accelerated progression if someone significantly exceeds the norm.

There then develops an extremely complex system, sometimes maintained by the supervisor, but more frequently by the Personnel Department, which automatically generates reports, letters etc. In either case it is time consuming, bureaucratic and frequently disregarded by both management and employees, often because the reports take so long to reach the supervisor that the lateness complained of has long since passed. If the supervisor does act in such situations, the defence is often that the employee has been 'on time' since the offending period or, if a letter is given, it is regarded as a battle honour by the employee concerned. It is not unknown for employees to play the system and collect large numbers of warning letters, but just stay on the right side of being suspended.

When investigating UK practice, Continental found a number of companies, which at that time had introduced single status in most areas, but had retained clocking for manual workers – British Fermentation Products, The Associated Octel Company, Sony (UK) Ltd and Molins Ltd. Scottish Timber Products started in a greenfields situation in 1973 without time clocks, but found that the absence of time keeping arrangements made for consider-able problems with its continuous four shift system. A clocking system was introduced but with no automatic or rigid system for pay deductions in the event of lateness. Other companies had abolished clocking, including Hewlett Packard, (who even operated a flexitime system without time recording), IBM, Texas Instruments, British Broadcasting Corporation, Alcoa (UK) Ltd. at its Lynmouth smelter, G. D. Searle and H. P. Bulmer. Most of these companies combined 'no clocking' with a relaxed attitude to minor non-persistent lateness and reported few problems. In the Wrexham area, however, Continental found that clocking was the norm for manual workers.

It is, of course, possible to record attendance in other ways. A small number of companies use a signature book and some 10 per cent require the supervisor to keep a record. Some use both, a clock and a foreman's time sheet, paying by whichever is the later; others now use computerised recording systems which also calculate wages. However, for non-manual employees most companies do not record attendance at all. Continental found in its survey that about 40 per cent of administrative employees, 50 per cent of supervisors and 75 per cent of executives and 'professionals' did not have their attendance recorded in any way. Of those companies (about 20 per cent of the total), which used the same method of recording attendance for all employees, 25 per cent used a clock, six per cent a signature book, two per cent flexitime, 31 per cent had no record and the largest number, 35 per cent, used the supervisor's record.

With the general policy of common terms and conditions of employment, both Continental and Nissan were faced with the choice 'To clock or not to clock'. We also had to consider that if there was to be no clocking what alternative method of recording attendance should be used and what would be the attitude towards lateness.

Considering the latter first, both companies believed it to be of paramount importance that all staff developed the attitude that it was normal to get to work on time. In Continental's case, with its continuous process operation, one person has to hand over to the other and the employee who is scheduled to finish has to wait for his replacement to arrive. Frequently in such circumstances a knock for knock arrangement develops, but in order to develop the right attitude it was important to consider attendance on time as being the norm. Concurrent with this, however, management has to recognise that there are occasions on which employees, through no fault of their own, are unable to arrive on time. Often it can be said that the employee who is an hour late has made a

far greater effort to arrive than the person who is five minutes
late.

The key is the Supervisor. If the Supervisor and his staff have
the right relationship and everyone is properly motivated, good
timekeeping does not depend on a mechanistic form of time
recording but on the self-generated discipline within the group.
It was absolutely fundamental, to both the Continental and
Nissan philosophies, that the Supervisor should have responsibility for maintaining good timekeeping – not the clock with a
lateness control procedure administered by the Personnel Department. There is no substitute for the Supervisor knowing his
staff and having the ability to make decisions without reference
to an externally imposed bureaucratic procedure. To enable him
to make such decisions and take appropriate action, it is therefore
necessary for the Supervisor to maintain his own records. While
allowances can be made for the infrequent offender, it is also
essential that the frequent offender be dealt with. Thus, however
understanding the company might be to the vast majority of
employees it has to retain the ability both to stop pay, and to take
disciplinary action against those who abuse the system. And in a
company, which espouses common terms and conditions, that
policy applies not only on the shop floor but to supervisors,
engineers and administrators. Single status is not just about
giving manual workers the same conditions as white-collar
workers – it is also about applying common disciplines to all.

Thus Continental's policy on timekeeping was developed. The
specific clause of the Agreement with the TGWU states:

> The Company trusts its employees to act responsibly and to be
> at work on time to ensure a proper handover between
> shifts.... It also expects day workers to be at their place of
> work at their established starting time. The Company does not
> require any employee to use a time recording clock nor does it
> stop pay for infrequent short periods of lateness.

Nissan's paragraph, allowing for the fact that continuous shifts
were not being worked was identical, but in addition Nissan
included in its critical working practices paragraph a clause
which read:

> Employees will be prepared for work at their place of work at
> the start and end of the normal day/shift.

The place of work at the start of the day is not the clock or the changing room but the team's rest area where the Supervisor holds the start of shift meeting. Thus a supervisor knows immediately if he has any latecomers or absentees and is able to plan accordingly. He is not rushing around trying to do the jobs of people who are late.

Equally, at the break periods and at the end of shift, people work until the finishing time. If work standards are properly established, 'working ahead' and 'catching up' can only reduce quality. But certain practices do develop – for instance in Nissan, the rest areas contain boilers for tea making (and some groups have brought in their own refrigerators!) and each day, on a rota basis, one person has the job of making the tea a few minutes before break time so that everything is ready when required.

Such attitudes depend far more upon the approach and style of the managers and supervisors than they do upon what is written in the Agreement. Indeed, the best managers barely need to look at the written word. It is, however, necessary to retain the ability to be able to take action against those employees who abuse the trust. The formula developed in both companies was virtually identical.

> In the event of this trust being abused and the Company being dissatisfied with an employee's timekeeping record, he will be liable to be stopped pay and may be required to comply with a more rigorous form of timekeeping. He will also be liable to disciplinary action.

> Employees who are more than five minutes late will report to their Supervisor before commencing work. Employees who know they will be unavoidably late must notify the Company prior to the start of day or shift.

Thus both companies provided both the means of facilitating supervisory control over timekeeping, and also the mechanism for dealing with the employee who might abuse the system. The timekeeping paragraphs went further, however:

> In the event of overall timekeeping levels or patterns becoming unacceptable, the Company's policy of not requiring employees to use time recording clocks and not stopping pay for infrequent short periods of lateness may be reviewed at any time.

This meant, in fact, that this particular paragraph was not subject to the overall agreement which provided that any variations to the Agreement could only be discussed jointly and only be terminated with six months notice. Of course, in approaching such a position there would, no doubt, be discussions, but the wording meant that this paragraph could be unilaterally terminated if the companies so wished. One final clause in both companies' Agreement:

> The Company and the Union recognise that it is in the interest of all parties to minimise lateness and will work together in whatever way necessary to this end.

Thus, there was a recognition by all concerned, that we were moving down a very lightly trodden path, at least for the manual workers. While we had total confidence that with the right approach people would respond there was sufficient hesitancy – particularly at Continental – to make us introduce the caveats and controls. Indeed, at Continental, a time clock was installed to be used for overtime recording, but also to enable the 'more rigorous form of timekeeping' to be implemented if necessary.

In the event we need not have worried. After seven years, there simply is no lateness problem in Continental. The hand-over process works well, and while trade-offs do exist, they work primarily in the direction of people coming in early rather than late. There have, of course, been occasional individual situations, but these have been dealt with by the supervisors on an immediate basis by private discussion. No-one has had to be formally disciplined for lateness and at no time has the clock had to be used.

While earlier days, the same pattern has emerged at Nissan – there is no lateness problem. No only has a more rigorous timekeeping method not been needed, but by specific request of the supervisors, *no* clock has been installed. So confident are they of their ability to handle any situations that arise, that they feel no need for any mechanical system. Even for the recording of overtime they find it preferable to control it themselves, rather than rely on mechanistic systems.

If you have no clock you cannot queue at it!

The second concern in this area is absenteeism and, again, potential abuse by manual workers of a white-collar-type sickness benefit scheme ranks very high in the list of concerns raised by managements contemplating the single status route. Traditionally, in the UK, manual workers' sickness benefit schemes are considerably worse than those granted to 'staff' and the introduction of common terms and conditions inevitably means significant improvements for the former group.

While most companies give sickness benefit to non-manual employees from the day they join, a very few give a similar benefit to manual employees. In the can manufacturing industry Continental found that the benefits were significantly better for the non-manual worker, particularly with regard to the maximum length of time for which benefit is payable. Although in the last few years, many companies have made substantial strides towards harmonisation, the Engineering Employers Federation found in 1986[1] that at 32.1 per cent, sick pay schemes were the least likely of the fringe benefits to be harmonised.

In seeking to establish its policy, Continental referred to a number of sources. A 1973 study by the Department of Employment[2] concluded that the following factors *may* adversely affect absenteeism – an agency labour force, a female labour force, long journey to work, unmarried employees with few family responsibilities, high overtime levels, high income level, large plant and generous sick pay scheme. The study considered that length of service, shift patterns and physical working conditions had little effect on absence levels. However, the most important conclusion was that the quality of supervision was the one factor which could be isolated in determining the reasons for absenteeism.

Dr P. Taylor, Chief Medical Officer of the Post Office, published a paper in the *Journal of the Royal College of Physicians* in 1974,[3] and identified many of the Department of Employment factors as being influential on absence rates, but stated 'contrary to the belief of some managers, sick pay schemes have not been shown to increase absence, except for relatively short periods after substantial increases are introduced. The evidence fails to substantiate allegations that the level of social security and other benefits given during sickness, are an important cause of high rates of absence, except in a few of the lower paid.' Dr Taylor particularly highlighted job satisfaction as being an important factor. Lack of job satisfaction 'may not itself cause ill health, but it can certainly reduce a man's motivation to go out to work on a cold and rainy day, when he also happens to have a minor indisposition'.

There are many other studies and many of the conclusions are contradictory but a number of points of general agreement do emerge. These can be summed up by stating that absenteeism is generally lowest where there is a high degree of job satisfaction, where there is a supervisor able to positively motivate his working group, and where the group is small and well defined.

When studying the situation in the UK, Continental found that with the almost total absence of any legislation relating to company sickness benefit schemes, there was a wide range of practices in the UK. At one extreme was the practice of Parker Pen Company, which provided 90 per cent of salary (with three per cent compound interest per annum) until the employee retires and at the other extreme were companies which gave no benefit at all. It is an area however in which there were considerable improvements in the late 1970s, for the 1976 Prices and Incomes Policy permitted companies to make improvements to their sickness benefit schemes, without this being charged against the, then, five per cent limit on earnings increases.

To many, the question of the level of sickness benefit, is as much a moral as an economic issue. There is very little justification on moral grounds for the office worker having better sick pay than the manual worker. The employee who has to be absent for several weeks or months, is normally genuinely ill and to suggest that the manual worker who has had a heart attack should be paid for six weeks, while the salaried worker with the same condition is paid for six months or more, is unjustifiable. Indeed an argument could be constructed that if a differential is to exist it should favour the manual worker. The absence problem in industry is not the worker who is genuinely ill and has to be away for months, but the employee, white- or blue-collar, who regularly takes two or three days off.

The one authoritative study showing the actual levels of absenteeism throughout the country is the government's *General Household Survey*.[4] Taking occupational groups, and giving 1983 figures, the 1985 Survey showed the following absences for sickness and 'personal and other reasons':

Managers   4.5 per cent
Professionals   3   per cent

Intermediate non-manual	5	per cent
Junior non-manual	5	per cent
Foremen and Supervisors	6	per cent
Skilled manual	7	per cent
Semi-skilled manual	8	per cent
Unskilled manual	7	per cent

The groups that are most likely to be paid when absent are the managers and professionals. The groups least likely to be paid are the manual workers. But the evidence is that absenteeism is in fact highest among those least likely to be paid – the manual workers at 7 or 8 per cent, against 3 or 4 per cent for professionals and managers.

In spite of this evidence, or perhaps because of lack of knowledge of it, there remains the suspicion that the manual worker will abuse an improved sickness benefit scheme. Thus for a company considering common terms and conditions, the issue of sickness benefit is one of the toughest decisions to make, for no-one has seriously contemplated reducing the staff scheme to the level of that of the manual workers. Indeed in an established company, where the sickness benefit scheme forms part of the employment contract, it would be a breach of contract to do so without joint agreement, and that is hardly likely to be forthcoming.

As with timekeeping, both, Continental and Nissan – and the many other companies who have now gone down this route – took the view that the essential point was to establish the philosophy that all employees are to be trusted. Again, however, it remains necessary to be able to deal with the people who abuse that trust. We took the view that short-period sickness absenteeism has little to do with sickness and a lot to do with motivation and commitment. The reason why managers and professionals are more likely to come to work when they are sick is not simply that the physical pressures of the job are less, but that they are more motivated. If you are committed to your job, you will try harder to do it. Thus the whole package developed by such companies is much the most important aspect in keeping absence down to low levels.

Both companies therefore declared it as their intention that 'employees who are genuinely ill should not be significantly better off nor significantly worse off financially than had they

been working the basic hours'. And the sickness benefit provided
rose in Continental's case to a maximum of six months benefit on
'full pay', after five years service, but Nissan significantly
improved on this with benefit rising to 12 months on full pay after
twelve months service. These levels are generous, but the view is
that companies have to be more concerned about the employee
who is off for two days, than they do about the employee who is
off for six months – for the latter will be genuinely ill and the
former may be 'swinging it'.

In order to control the potential abuser of the sickness benefit
schemes, the mechanistic controls put in included requirements
that

– all employees must notify the company, prior to the start of
  work, that they will be absent.

– all appropriate certificates must be submitted.

– absentees must report to their supervisor on return to work.

– the company maintains the right to refer the employee to his
  doctor, if there is a pattern of absence, if absence is due to a
  recurring health problem or is prolonged, and in such cases
  payment may be delayed.

– if the company is dissatisfied with an employee's record, or if it
  is satisfied that there is abuse or misrepresentation, the
  employee will be disqualified from receiving sickness benefit
  and may be subject to disciplinary action.

– in all cases sickness benefit for the first five days is at the
  company's discretion.

– in the event of the overall levels of sickness absence, or
  patterns becoming unacceptable, the company reserves the
  right to review the sickness benefit scheme at any time.

On top of this, however, both the TGWU in Continental's case
and the AEU in Nissan's recognised the generosity of the
schemes and both formally agreed that 'The Company and the
Union recognise that it is in the interests of all parties to keep
absenteeism to a minimum and will work together, in whatever
way necessary, to this end.'

Thus, both Nissan and Continental, in providing a good

scheme for all, recognised that the essential control mechanism was the supervisor, that there had to be control to avoid abuse and to deal with those who did abuse the scheme, and that it was essential to have the union support policy.

In Continental the scheme worked as desired. Levels of absenteeism have been consistently low and are generally around two per cent. This is a level any employer would be delighted with, and it has been achieved, not by having to implement the mechanistic controls, but by allowing the supervisors full responsibility for controlling their sections, and by doing everything to provide meaningful interesting jobs and a commitment to their company.

As with lateness, sickness absenteeism in Nissan is remarkably low and is around the 3 per cent level. It is affected, not only by the motivation of staff, but also by the fact that the workforce is young and all have undergone a stringent medical examination before being accepted. Nevertheless, when compared with typical motor industry practice, where managers are pleased to get down to ten per cent, and where attendance bonuses have to be used to persuade employees that it is worth coming to work, it is no mean achievement.

But what happens when people are sick? Without doubt one of the most significant decisions for both Continental and Nissan was to offer private medical insurance to all employees.

Companies normally only provide this facility to directors and senior managers. An IDS Survey published in 1984[5] found only five companies (Rank Xerox, Sun Life, Potterton International, Hambro Life and Taylor Instruments) out of 36 surveyed offering company paid schemes to all employees and four out of these five specified lengthy periods of service before employees could join. The EETPU has negotiated a number of schemes for manual workers but they remain very much in the minority – even though at the end of 1983, IDS estimated that total membership of such schemes was around 4.3 million people. While total membership appears to have plateaued after the spectacular growth of the 1970s such schemes have a virtually untapped source – manual workers – in which to market their services.

Private medical insurance is a political hot potato and certainly when Continental was considering its options the debate was at its peak. The Labour government's decision to phase out pay beds in NHS hospitals had resulted in a sharp reduction from around 4300 in 1976 to less than 2700 in 1979. The incoming Conservative government had announced in the Queen's Speech a Bill to facilitate the wider use of private medical care. The Health Service unions were threatening to withdraw services to newly admitted private patients and NUPE stated they would 'black' all pay beds from 1980 unless the government previously removed them. Not the most tranquil of moments to make a decision!

For Continental and subsequently Nissan the argument was not political – nor was it about the respective merits of NHS versus private treatment. It was essentially about common terms and conditions of employment. Continental had made the decision, as did Nissan, that to be competitive at the senior level private medical insurance had to be part of its employment package. If it is serious about common terms and conditions the logic points to extending that arrangement to all staff. It is as simple as that.

However, no trade union, apart from the EEPTU, can agree to private medical insurance as part of a negotiated package. Indeed, as it is a taxable benefit, there are many employees who, not wishing to use the service, would object to the company paying a premium on their behalf and thus subjecting them to a tax liability.

Not wishing either to embarrass the trade unions by seeking to persuade them to agree or to put them in a position of having to refuse to agree, both companies decided that private medical insurance would be totally outside the negotiations. It was therefore offered to employees on an individual and voluntary basis. No trade union has agreed to private medical insurance and no employee has a tax liability for a benefit he does not wish to use. The companies offer a non-contractual benefit under which private medical insurance for employees and their families is paid for by the company.

When commentators speak glibly of 'single status', issues of this type are easily forgotten. But companies also have to consider what happens when an employee runs out of sickness benefit. This is not necessarily the end of the employee's connection with the Company. However, in many organisations it is, and once benefit has expired, then frequently the employee will leave the Company, or if he has had a sufficiently long service will be able to take early retirement. According to the

National Association of Pension Funds Surveys, 99 per cent of companies provide some method of protecting employees who become permanently unable to work. This takes many forms and most provide for early retirement with a pension related to potential service rather than actual service. One problem with actually retiring somebody on pension is that it is somewhat inflexible and there is a distinct possibility that an employee who has retired on an ill-health pension may subsequently find he is capable of working. Very few companies are willing to rehire an employee who has retired on these grounds, but the alternative is that the ex-employee will be in receipt of both an ill-health pension, and a wage from a new employer. While this may be in the interest of the ex-employee, there does appear to be a certain injustice, as far as the previous employer (or rather the previous pension scheme) is concerned.

When reviewing the alternatives available, both Continental and Nissan decided to go down the Permanent Health Insurance route (perhaps it should more properly be called Permanent Ill-Health Insurance). PHI is established via an insurance company, whereby for a given premium paid by the Company, the employee receives a benefit from the date his normal sickness benefit expires to the time he is scheduled for normal retirement, dies or is able to resume work. The benefit may be for any amount related to previous salary, but the Continental and Nissan decision was that it should be related to fifty per cent of final salary, including the State Disability Benefit. The benefit is normally increased on an annual basis, and the insurance company pays to the Company an amount, sufficient to allow for continuing payments into the pension scheme, on behalf of the employee. If the employee survives until normal retirement age, he would then be paid a pension related to the insurance benefit he would be receiving at the time.

Although a highly visible and much appreciated benefit, the cost of such schemes is comparatively cheap – probably due to the fact that the insurance company actuaries have calculated that beneficiaries rarely claim the benefit for very long periods.

In conclusion then, there is little to be frightened of in introducing generous sickness benefits for manual workers – provided it is part of a well thought out package, embracing all aspects of employment and that control is where it should be – with the immediate supervisor. Failing this strategic approach, this is one area in which it is easy to perceive of a situation where the Company can get all of the costs and few of the potential benefits. But with the right strategy success can be achieved and all the fears will be found to be unfounded.

8 Evaluation, Payment, and Appraisal – Servants, not Masters

In established organisations both large and small, job evaluation and the systems and processes on which it depends and to which it leads are an accepted part of everyday life. As part of the job evaluation process companies have constructd job descriptions and specifications, grading structures, grading grievance procedures, review panels etc; There is little doubt as to why job evaluation is generally considered desirable. Its main objective is to provide a systematic method of establishing internal relativities which can then be used as a basis for determining relative pay levels.

Unfortunately, like many good ideas which are simple in concept, the execution has become complex and in many cases the process has become an end in itself. The preservation of the integrity of the job evaluation system has, in many cases, become more important than the tasks actually being carried out. The process often results in many hours of work discussing the detail of a vast range of jobs, preparing job descriptions which are written down, agreed at various levels, analysed, rated, weighted, grieved etc.

Numerous consultant-inspired proprietory methods of job evaluation have been produced. Listed by IDS in its *Job Evaluation Review*[1] are the following.

The Hay Guide Chart Profile Method
Inbucon – Direct Consensus and Pay Points
Urwick Orr – The Profile Method
PA – Factor Forced Pair Method
Institute of Advisory Management – Office Job Evaluation
Wyatt Company (UK) Ltd – Employee Points Factor Comparison
Arthur Young – Decision Band Method
TPF & C – Job Evalution Toolkit
Brunel University – Weight of Responsibility
Alan Jones – Paired Comparison

In addition 50 consultants are listed as providing a job evaluation service.

There is little doubt that there is a job evaluation industry which comprises not only the consultants but also vast numbers of in-house professionals whose task is continually to fine-tune and update the system. But unfortunately the end result is a rigid structure which restricts what people can do, which delays response to changing technology and increases the time it takes for companies to react to changing market conditions, both for its products and its people. There are examples in virtually every company of people refusing to take on additional or changed work because 'it is not in my job description' or of the company having difficulty in hiring scarce talents because the job evaluates at a lower level than the market place salary demands. Job evaluation often results in very fine distinctions between jobs, with a resulting multigrade salary structure with considerable salary overlaps. Thus it becomes possible to earn the same salary at several different grade levels. The preservation of the system becomes more important than reacting rapidly to change – in short the tail begins to wag the dog.

This problem has long been recognised. In 1968 the National Board for Prices and Incomes stated in its study on job evaluation 'management thought the inflexibility of job evaluation schemes to be their greatest disadvantage'[2] The Work Research Unit's paper 'Job evaluation and changing technology'[3] highlights many of the factors putting pressure on job evaluation systems – changing technology, work restructuring, employment structures and changing occupational skills, the move from 'one man one job', and the development of teamwork.

Later, in 1985, the Work Research Unit reporting the conclusion of an Amsterdam conference 'Innovation in Work and Pay'[4] stated 'Job evaluation imposes rigidities. Job evaluation systems, with analytical systems still predominant, have the effect of bureaucratising pay management and can hinder the introduction of new work'. The report lists a number of developments which attempt to overcome these problems. Included are

– avoiding detailed specific job descriptions
– developing universal systems capable of covering all levels in the organisation
– re-examining the validity of such factors as 'formal training'

when in a time of rapid change continuous training is more
important
- giving separate treatment to 'working conditions' because they
inhibit job redesign
- growing use of simplified approaches to cope with change
- providing for multi-skilled work
- eliminating sex bias

Of course, it is not possible to eliminate job evaluation entirely –
nor would it be desirable to do so for inter-job comparisons are
made constantly on an informal basis even where a formal system
does not exist. Every time we say that a Managing Director's job is
worth more than a manager's or a craftsman has a more difficult
job than a semi-skilled operator, we are making an inter-job
comparison. Such comparisons are easy to make and readily
understood. Difficulties arise, however, when we try to compare,
say, engineers who are doing broadly similar types of work and
the system attempts to distinguish varying degrees of complexity.
Unfortunately work does not arrive in discrete lumps which can
be described as 'more complex', 'complex' or 'less complex'. In
any one task there will be elements of each level of complexity
and at any one time it can well happen that a senior person could
be doing work of a lesser complexity than a junior.

While job evaluation is generally regarded as being systematic
it can in no way be regarded as objective – at least in how it is
initially structured. For the key to any system is the selection of
the factors to be considered and the weighting to be given to
those factors. There can be little doubt that once a system is
established it is in the interest of management to administer the
scheme objectively. But the scheme has to be initially structured
to give the results that the people covered by it perceive to be fair.
In fact it does not really matter what scheme is used as long as the
results are broadly acceptable to employees and it helps management to recruit, motivate and retain staff of the right calibre. As
the Work Research Unit paper points out 'The choice of weighting
is likely to be affected by the considerations as to how acceptable
to all the parties involved the resultant rank order of jobs is likely
to be, and this will be influenced by such things as the different
degrees of unions strength and organisation, and historical wage
relationships'. To be successful a job evaluation scheme must give
the result people feel to be fair.

It was against this background of dissatisfaction with existing job evaluation practices that Continental management considered the ranking order of jobs within the company. The position was complicated by the company's desire to establish a fully inte-grated grading structure combining all occupations – manual, administrative, supervisory and engineering. The view was that common terms and conditions of employment means among other things a common grading structure. But also an integrated structure is an essential element in creating the environment in which the divisions between white- and blue-collar no longer exist, individuals can be given greater responsibility and career paths can be considerably broadened. Even now this is rare.

Thornton's Chocolates has operated an integrated grading structure covering all employees below Board level since the 1960s. Hewlett Packard, Digital and National Semi-conductor in the electronics field, have gone down this route. In the more traditional industries, Cummins Engines and Pilkington Insula-tion combined their movement to integrated pay structures with other radical changes towards greater flexibility and harmonisa-tion. In its study of such systems[5] Industrial Relations Services clearly indicated that no organisation was introducing the practice without other significant changes, but concluded that it was too early to properly assess the implications and problems associated with the change.

In Continental, the initial 'Occupational Grade Structure' – totally integrated – was created by three people sitting round a table, using what would probably be termed 'informal whole job comparison'. It was nevertheless decided that, after two or three years operation, a more formal analysis might be needed. Thus, in late 1982, it was agreed to examine the structure on a more analytical basis to see if changes were needed. Continental undertook a review of the proprietory schemes and, despite claims that some were capable of covering the full spectrum of occupations, decided that in its environment none of these schemes were suitable. (Since that time several of the better known systems have undertaken further development work and Hay in particular has been used by Pilkington across the whole range of its jobs). Continental decided therefore to enlist the help of ACAS in producing a factor/points evaluation scheme which would apply to all occupations but at the same time would not inhibit the flexibility it had achieved.

The detailed process which took a year has been fully described by Industrial Relations Services[6] but was based on responsibility (four sub-divisions), education and knowledge, training and familiarisation, initiative, ingenuity and effort. A total of 1000 points was determined and each factor assigned a proportion of this total, depending on its importance.

While this task proved comparatively easy the preparation of job descriptions was more difficult, for the principle of flexibility meant that there were few jobs rigidly definable in the traditional way. It was therefore decided to keep the definitions as simple as possible, concentrate on the main functions but ensure that the other skills and responsibilities were properly accounted for. In the usual way each job description was agreed and signed by all concerned and each member of the Committee then evaluated the job.

The committee was concerned that the scheme they had put together would result in major upset of the relationships that had been established and to which employees had become accustomed. But after some adjustment to factor definition the results of a pilot test came out in line with the 'feel' of what was right. With this under its belt the evaluation committee started the full evaluation process and, at the conclusion of the job description stage, went through the assessment process. The results compared to the original round table evaluation are shown below (note the addition of a new bottom grade).

Original		*Evaluated*
A	–	Juniors/Re-workers/ Temporary employees
B	Janitor/Driver	Janitor/Driver Receptionist/Typist
C	Operator	Operator
	Clerks	Clerks
	Secretary/Receptionist	Stores Controller
D	Q A Inspector	Q A Inspector
		Secretary
E1	Trainee Maintainer	Trainee Maintainer
E2	Production Maintainer	Production Maintainer
	Fitter Maintainer	Fitter Maintainer
	Electrician	Electrician

	Tooling Inspector	Tooling Inspector
		Assistant Buyer
E3	Lead Maintainer	Lead Maintainer
F	Buyer	Buyer
	Accountant Supervisor	Accountant Supervisor
	Customer Service Engineer	Customer Service Engineer
	Personnel and Training Officer	Personnel and Training Officer
G	Shift Superintendent	Shift Superintendent
H	Shift Manager	Shift Manager
		Project Engineer
I	Electrical Engineer	Electrical Engineer
	Mechanical Engineer	Mechanical Engineer

NOTES (I) There were a number of minor job title changes and in all cases the revised title is used. This makes no difference to the ranking order.

(II) In the original listing grade numbers were used. The table above is based on the revised nomenclature but again this makes no difference to the ranking.

As can be seen, one or two new job titles have been added but the only real difference is the downgrading of the receptionist and the upgrading of the secretary. Originally it was intended that the two would be interchangeable but in practice this did not happen. Therefore the not unexpected result was a moving apart of the two positions. Thus as stated by the Industrial Relations Services report of the exercise, 'the exercise largely justified the original structure implemented in 1980'.[7] This is not surprising; as already stated job evaluation *has* to produce results which are 'felt fair' by those affected.

It should be a salutary reminder to the experts and consultants that the original evaluation was determined by two or three people in a few hours. The systematic job evaluation took a dozen people a year. The changes necessary, because of jobs being done in a different way to that envisaged, could have been concluded by the original group in a few minutes. Flexible working practices simply do not need complex job evaluation.

To a large extent the Continental grading structure reflected traditional thinking and while it did break new ground its antecedents are clearly recognisable. Between Continental and Nissan however a conceptual step change took place.

Learning from Continental, Nissan determined to go even further in simplicity and regarded what came to be called its 'Occupational Classification' as fundamental to the objective of achieving flexibility. Thus in the Agreement the only reference to job titles is 'All employees covered by these Agreements will be placed in one of the occupational classifications shown in the Appendix. This in no way detracts from the agreements on flexibility'.

To maximise flexibility it is necessary to minimise the number of job titles and to make them as general as possible. It is helpful to reduce to the lowest possible level the number of layers between the top and bottom of the hierarchy. In studying the tasks performed in the manufacture of automobiles we became convinced that the British motor industry had an excessive number of levels. Taking into account both manual and white-collar occupations Ford has 15 different levels below manager and Austin Rover 19; Massey Ferguson had 44 grades in three structures for its white collar workers (a job evaluation exercise has been held to reduce these to 6 to 8). Within these levels there are scores of different job titles. In Nissan all tasks are covered by 15 job titles, covering Managing Director to Administrative Assistants and, within the Production Department, it takes but six steps to go from Managing Director to Manufacturing Staff – Managing Director, Director, Manager, Senior Supervisor, Supervisor, Team Leader, Manufacturing Staff.

Nissan has no job descriptions and no numbered grades – numbered grades rapidly lead to claims for higher grades and result in the phenomenon of grade drift.

Everyone at the same level in the hierarchy is of the same status. Thus there is at present only one level of Manager and all are simply called 'Manager'. Equally so with Engineers. Nissan does not employ Production Engineers, Design Engineers, Process Engineers, Industrial Engineers, etc. – it employs 'Engineers'. Of course, people work in Departments but there is no organisational impediment to moving across. Especially important is the fact that Engineers, Supervisors and Controllers are at the same level in the organisation. This both reflects the view that all of these positions are of equal importance and again facilitates movement.

It is recognised that often the work done by people in different levels in the organisation will overlap. Thus at any one point in time the Engineer may be undertaking more complex work than the Senior Engineer. The difference is that the Senior Engineer or Senior Controller is in charge of a group of Engineers.

Administrative Assistant is the generic title given to those people undertaking clerical, secretarial and receptionist work. Controller is the name of professionals working in the indirect areas – purchasing, finance, personnel etc. With all of these the concept has been to broaden responsibilities and enhance flexibility and thus retreat from the straitjacket of rigid job evaluation and its associated techniques. All people doing secretarial work are at the same level. There really can be no justification in the British tradition of paying more to the secretaries of senior bosses.

Nissan's manufacturing operation in the United States, in Smyrna, Tennessee, has shown the possibility of running a plant with two types of manual worker called by them Production Technicians and Maintenance Technicians. While the NMUK terminology is different – Technician and Manufacturing Staff – the number remains the same. The question of titles is in fact important. We were clear that production work with Nissan would be different and wanted to get away from the general concept of production staff being second-class citizens. Thus the normal titles of production worker, operator etc. were denied to us. We also wanted a title that could apply to everybody, for in a British environment there is a danger that anything which can be divisive will be. Our title became Manufacturing Staff – not perhaps ideal but suggestive of both the role and the responsibilities and, importantly, it is infinitely flexible.

With the occupational classification in place there comes the question of salaries. The logic of common terms and conditions means not only that there should be an integrated occupational classification but also that the method of payment should be the same. Until the 1986 Wages Act the manual worker who wished to be paid in 'coin of the realm' was fully protected by the 1831 Truck Act. He had the right to be paid in cash, while the white-collar worker received payment via a monthly salary credited directly to a bank or other nominated institution. In this the British worker is unlike his continental counterpart. In Germany the public sector and nationalised industries had changed nearly all manual workers to monthly status by the late 1970s and over 80 per cent of French workers are paid monthly.

In the UK, not only is the method of payment different, but the salary and wage structures are at variance. Most white-collar workers are on annual salaries within a salary range. Progression along this range, whether on a time or merit basis, is regarded as the norm. Manual workers are invariably paid the rate for the job. While there may be differences in earnings due to payment by results or bonus systems there is little room for variations in the basic pay. Trade unions have traditionally sought to achieve a 'going rate' for each job and argue that each employee should receive this irrespective of ability. Different levels of basic pay are regarded as divisive, and any form of progression apart from fixed service increments, is believed to lead to injustice and the development of the 'blue-eyed boy' syndrome. Their philosophy has been to protect the inefficient rather than reward the efficient. In those many companies where payment by results systems operate, often artificial limitations on earnings are established and 'understood' by other employees and managers.

The New Earnings Survey on 'Payment by Results in Britain', 1968-82,[8] showed that in 1982 some 45 per cent of adult men in manufacturing industry had some form of PBR applied to them. The arguments in favour of and against PBR systems are well known but in the changing management environment of the late 1980s and in particular in light of the emphasis on the role of the supervisor the Work Research Unit has stated 'PBR puts the worker in business for himself and he can thus pit himself against the broad interests of the company; that PBR symbolises managers' lack of confidence in employees' will to work and employees' ability to manage their own work'.[9]

At the other end of the scale are plant and company-wide schemes such as the Scanlon Plan (which relates total wages to total sales value), Added Value (in which the increase in added value above a certain level triggers an additional payment) and the Rucker Plan (which relates wages to added value). All of these schemes are complex and the direct effect on individual performance is limited because of the inability of the individual to relate effort or achievement to reward. And this is the paradox in any system which relates effort or achievement to reward. To be directly successful the individual must be able to directly influence earning power but if this is possible many other variables come into play which, if taken into account, (and to make the system 'fair' they should be) necessarily make the system more complex and thus less easy to relate achievement to reward. Thus within each system there lies the seeds of its own destruction – or at the very least it needs a complex maintenance process to reinforce the motivational element. It was somewhat ironic that during the 1986 pay negotiations Austin Rover introduced a 'quality bonus' for its manual workers while at exactly the same time Leyland Vehicles negotiated out its quality bonus because of difficulties in achieving satisfactory measurements.

There are, however, many pressures causing employers to think about the need for different payment structures. As we have seen in Chapter 1, new technology is blurring the differences between white-collar and blue-collar jobs. Manual workers are increasingly moving away from tasks where they can directly influence production levels. Robotics, computer controlled machine tools and line-paced operations combine with teamworking, flexibility and the emphasis on quality to minimise the need for payment systems which enable the employee to directly influence output.

For both Continental and Nissan the question of the method of salary payment had a great significance. Again, common terms and conditions of employment means a single means of paying the money. It was in fact unthinkable to pay everyone a weekly wage in a pay packet, thus it became annual salaries for all. But even more important the method of payment has a symbolic significance. Probably the first and most immediately obvious difference seen by the potential candidate when reading the advertisement in a newspaper, is that the job has an annual salary. In terms used by the diplomats 'it is a signal that things are different'.

Despite dire warnings to the contrary, neither company in practice had any difficulty with this aspect of its employment package. A small number of new starters, particularly those who were unemployed immediately prior to joining, needed a short period to adjust but both companies did whatever was necessary to assist. In fact, employees joined Nissan, not only with an annual salary, but also a salary with progression along that range being related to merit, for the agreement states 'A salary range will be establishd to apply to each occupational classification and progression through this range will be related to the individual's performance'. In this, Nissan, if not unique, is a member of a very exclusive group of companies. Again, heading the listing, came the electronics and computing companies. Hewlett Packard, Digital, National Semi-conductors and IBM. To these can now be added Sanyo and Inmos. In IBM all employees are rated at one of four performance levels dependent on the degree to which they meet or exceed the requirements of the job. Salary progression and the maximum level attainable is then related to the performance level. Hewlett Packard, with salary ranges of at least 35 per cent, relates progression to a combination of performance appraisal and ranking against comparable staff. Inmos allows two pay rises per year – the general increase in January and a management-determined merit increase in July. Very few companies, who are actively pursuing single status, have bitten the 'merit increase for manual workers' bullet! Industrial Relations Services, when commenting on the practice,[10] did not find it to be widespread nor did it believe that it would grow significantly except on greenfield sites. Perhaps this is true and it does not particularly matter except that if a company is to be true to the logic of common terms and conditions then the *same* system must be applied to all whatever that system might be.

When devising a payment system it has to be appreciated that management and staff may have different perceptions of the objectives of the system. To managers it needs to enable the company to recruit, motivate and retain staff of the required calibre, while containing costs to a level which maintains overall competitiveness. To employees the system may be used to increase rewards – their viewpoint is often shorter and more concerned with 'jam today'. The need is to reconcile the possible conflicting objectives and construct a system that works for the company rather than against it. As in much else the ACAS Work Research Unit has attempted to grasp the practical effects of new thinking in employee relations. In establishing the objectives of a system suitable for both changing technology and management styles its publication *Progressive Payment Systems* suggests that salary structures need to be concerned with

– avoiding tying the payment system to a standard pattern of work

- changing the emphasis from rewarding effort to rewarding results
- facilitating the introduction of new jobs or job redesign
- providing for the effects of pushing responsibility and decision making downwards
- providing for the development of broader skills, increased mobility and flexibility
- encouraging employees to become involved with customer needs particularly through improving quality and meeting delivery dates
- encouraging employees to give of their best by rewarding 'above standard' performance

A tall order!

However, when establishing the system two other golden rules need to be taken into account. First

Keep it simple

Second, and particularly for salary progression systems which depend on individual performance

Be fair and be *seen* to be fair

And being fair means having a system of measuring performance which in itself is fair.

The issue was put succinctly in *Progressive Payment Systems*. 'Any increase in the incidence of salary structures based on matching pay to individual performance, whether in the private or public sectors, is likely to bring to the fore the sometimes contentious issue of appraisal or merit rating schemes which often go with these structures ... they often attract suspicion because they are perceived as secretive and subjective. They can also often become ill-co-ordinated because of lack of management discipline leading to disparities in reward for what might be similar performance ... there is a lack of confidence in the fairness of the procedures used. A prime task will therefore be to ensure that when these schemes are used they are agreed between managers, employees and the recognised trade unions; that they are as open as possible, that they can be seen to be fair and that subjectivity is reduced to a minimum'.[11]

Any salary progression system depends very much on the

assessment of the individuals. Nissan therefore made the decision that its appraisal system would apply to everyone in the company. Again in this, while not unique, it is rare in British industry for systematic appraisal to be applied to all. However, the use of appraisals for manual workers is growing. The IPM's 1986 survey of appraisal systems[12] found that 24 per cent of respondent companies applied performance appraisal to manual workers compared with 2 per cent in 1977. This figure, however, probably exaggerates the use, for as in most surveys it is the more sophisticated companies that respond. Before much further expansion is undertaken, however, there needs to be a fundamental review of the quality of appraisal systems. Too often they are simply not up to the job they are asked to do. They are too complex, take up too much management time and frequently the only use to which they are put is as a reference document for the next review. There is a great tendency to over-rate – 'Average' is unacceptable, everybody has to be at least 'Above average'. They often reflect more on the ability of the appraiser to write English than on the qualities of the subject and frequently one or two factors determine the whole assessment. They look backwards not forwards and pay little attention to training and development needs.

In order to avoid these pitfalls an appraisal system has to be much more than a tool for objectively measuring performance. If designed and used effectively it can become the basis of a programme aimed at developing the human resources of the company, thus ensuring a constant flow of talent. An objective method of assessing performance against previous targets is a necessary but not sufficient means of achieving this goal. In addition the appraisal system has to identify both strengths and weaknesses and establish training and development programmes designed to build on strengths and eliminate weaknesses. It has also to highlight those areas of the organisation where replacement problems are likely to occur and thus warn the company, in sufficient time, to take remedial action.

Management by Objectives has gone through various phases of enthusiasm but there can be little doubt that, whatever phraseology is used, performance can best be assessed if it is measured against some previously established target. Such objectives must be agreed between the boss and the subordinate – they must be jointly owned, not imposed. They must be tough but achievable during the review period. It is not enough to ask the individual simply to do the job he is paid to do but equally the objectives must not be so far out of sight that no-one stands any chance of success. That is demotivating. They must be measurable – not expressed in vague terms such as 'Improve the level of absentee-ism' but 'Reduce absenteeism from 5.8 per cent to 4.8 per cent in the next six months'. (It is interesting that in Japan objectives are set so high that they are generally *unachievable*. The individual is assessed on effort and progress rather than attainment).

Nissan decided that every employee in the company should have objectives – there was to be no cut-off point – and as an important part of the appraisal each employee would be mea-sured against those objectives. Clearly the more constrained the job an individual does the more specific the objectives and at manufacturing staff level it became necessary to have much more uniformity between individuals than is necessary at manager level. The important point however is that *everyone* has objectives. Again, an element that the simplistic concept of single status overlooks.

In a mature organisation it is best that at management level the objective-setting period should be concentrated within a specified period of the year – probably the first three months of the calendar or financial year. This enables the company to develop a cohesion which would not be possible if the exercise were to be spread out throughout the year. Ideally the objectives for everyone should also be set at this time but practically this is rarely possible. The process does take time and in large organisations it probably works better to spread out the objectives of people below managerial level to coincide with the appraisal date.

Every company which hs an appraisal system has developed its own format applicable to its own circumstances and objec-tives. There is no one best system but there are many that are bad and thus fall into disrepute. This is bad enough when the appraisal is used to comment on performance and determine training needs but when it is a factor in determining pay increases then it becomes imperative that the appraisal is seen as being both objective and fair. Thus Nissan, in preparing its appraisal form, involved not only managers who would use it but also members of the Company Council who would be affected by it – as a result of which many beneficial changes were made.

As indicated in the indictment, many appraisal systems depend on the ability of the appraiser (the 'father') to write decent English. They also suffer from the halo effect, whereby the appraiser concentrates on a small number of factors which colour the whole process. In order to eliminate these problems and introduce as much objectivity as possible, it is necessary to eliminate the open-ended narrative appraisal, certainly for the 'non-manager' group. This means moving to a 'tick box' type of system but again these have many problems for frequently the box description is of the type which requires 'Outstanding, Above average, Average, Below Average, Poor' (or whatever definition is closest) to be ticked. In order to minimise these problems a number of actions are possible:

- the number of boxes should be irregular
- the order should not always be ascending left to right
- the box description should be written according to the factor being measured
- in all cases there should be room for a narrative addition if necessary.

This leads, for example, to a ranking order under the heading 'Teamworking':

- Always seeks to involve others
- Works well as a team member
- Makes a good effort
- Dislikes teamworking
- A total loner

'Teamworking', along with three other factors that are measured, Job Knowledge, Quality of Work and Flexibility, reflect the key characteristics NMUK included in its original advertising. Thus, not only are these factors aimed for in general terms but in measuring achievement they are at the top of the list which includes some fourteen other factors, the vast majority of which are applicable to all staff irrespective of occupation.

There then comes the all-important question of ratings, for not only are these to be used as basis for formally assessing performance and determining potential, but they are also to be a factor in determining merit pay. If costs are to be controlled it becomes doubly important that rating drift does not develop. This is the phenomenon equivalent to grade drift where, over a period of time, the ratings creep up. 'Average' becomes un-acceptable and everyone becomes 'Above average'. While a slight positive skewing in the rating distribution curve is acceptable on the basis that the selection process should have eliminated the potentially poor performer, a company should rate its staff according to its own standards and not those of an ouside organisation which employs people of a generally lower standard.

The key therefore in any rating system is to get the definitions right and in particular the middle rating into which the vast majority will fall has to be 'acceptable'. One such definition is:

Fully Proficient – Fully acceptable performance. Normal objectives met and assignments properly handled.

Above this comes 'Highly Commendable' and 'Outstanding' and below it 'Marginal' and 'Unsatisfactory'.

Thus it *is* possible to develop an appraisal system which can apply to all occupations and it *is* possible to construct an occupational classification and merit system that also applies to all. If one believes that all employees should be treated the same, the will can find a way. This approach is now well established within Nissan. Although most white-collar workers are well used to appraisal systems in previous employments the same cannot be said for manual workers. However, once having gone through the process and recognising that it can be fair, objective and helpful, Nissan's manufacturing staff have come to appreciate its benefits. Certainly in a rapidly growing company with many opportunities for promotion it greatly assists identifying people with potential who may need to gain in experience before such promotion can be offered. As important, job evaluation, the salary structure and appraisal system *can* become the servant rather than the master, can be responsive rather than dictatorial and can help, not hinder, a company in achieving its objectives.

9 The Union Question

The issue of union recognition was, in Nissan's early days, always at the forefront of media questioning. So it was with Nissan management. Indeed, with any inward investor a comprehensive review of labour relations in the various potential locations forms a significant part of the investment decision-making process. And, inevitably, the issue of whether or not to opt for trade union recognition comes to the fore.

There are over 2000 manufacturing companies with more than 500 employees in the UK. Of these only some 20 can be described as non-union in the sense that the company does not formally bargain with a trade union and about half a dozen of the 20 can be said to be part-unionised. Most of the non-union companies are household names – National Cash Register, Nestlé, IBM, Mars, Hewlett Packard, Black & Decker, Avon, Gillette, Texas Instruments and Revlon among them. Predominantly these large non-union companies are American-owned and a significant proportion are in the new technology sector employing large numbers of highly skilled graduates and a high proportion of female employees engaged on light assembly work. Both groups are among those least inclined towards trade union membership.

No doubt this preponderance of American-owned companies is a reflection of their practices back home. In particular in the last few years there has been a distinct trend among American managements investing in new facilities to locate their plants on the West Coast and the Southern States where, in particular, State 'Right to Work' legislation positively encourages non-unionism. This factor, combined with the decline in privately owned manufacturing industry in the US has resulted in a situation in which only about 18 per cent of the workforce is unionised and membership loss since 1982 has been around 2½ million.

As in many things British practices are following the American. The peak in trade union membership in the United Kingdom was in 1979 when some 13.2 million workers were paying subscriptions. By the end of 1985 membership had fallen to 10.8 million – a reduction of nearly 19 per cent.[1] Employment in this period reduced however by 'only' eight per cent, a contrast which emphasises the fact that it is those industries with a concentration of union membership that have declined the fastest.

It was however in the period approaching the peak of union membership – 1979 – that Continental was establishing itself. In fact from 1972 to 1979 there was an increase of 2½ million – perhaps the last ever sustained growth in union membership. While the decline in total membership continues there has been no significant change in the number of large non-union companies in the manufacturing sector. The chances of a unionised company opting for non-unionism are negligible and there are very few new companies with an initial employment of several hundred.

Potential inward investors have a view that British trade unionism will be a constraint on effective management. However this view is not limited to the UK. Toyota management when preparing for their joint manufacturing project with General Motors in Freemont, California came armed with a file of newspaper cuttings reporting the excesses of the UAW in that plant. They were persuaded to change their mind and today the Freemont plant is one of the most successful in General Motor's empire. In the UK, potential investors' adverse view of British trade unionism is related to the whole movement and not just specific sections. Thus the British trade union movement starts at a distinct disadvantage but, probably unknown to it, its biggest friend in gaining recognition is the British Industrial Relations Manager with whom it will be negotiating but who also understands the realities of life – what is and is not achievable.

A number of factors weigh in favour of trade union recognition. All employees have the legal right to belong or not to belong to a trade union and, whatever views an employer may have, there is nothing he can legally do to prevent employees joining a union (as opposed to recognising the union which is a different issue). Both Continental in North Wales and Nissan in the North-east were establishing themselves in areas with strong traditional links with the trade union and Labour movement. Many of the people recruited would be trade union members who would bring their membership with them – even if their unions were not recognised. In particular, craftsmen are loth to give up their membership, for while until very recently the days of many of the financial benefits have gone, the craft card remains to many a symbol of pride and achievement not to be tossed aside because of the whims of a particular employer – who, they perceive, may turn out to be transitory.

It was also important that trade union officials had been involved in discussions with the companies prior to the final decisions being made. Indeed the Northern Region TUC had taken the policy decision that were Nissan to select the North-east and determine that it wanted a single union deal then the unions not recognised would respect that decision. This, combined with the many statements welcoming the companies, would have meant that a non-union decision would have been a very real slap in the face and, almost certainly, would have been interpreted by the unions as a declaration of war.

Thus, both Continental and Nissan by going down this route would have been faced with a situation where, in strong union areas, union members would be recruited who very soon would have registered claims for union recognition – and would be denied such recognition. There was every chance of the cases becoming *causes célebres* and at the time Continental could have been taken down the ACAS route with a compulsory ballot and probably a final decision in favour of recognition. In the case of Nissan, with the Conservative government's legislative changes, that possibility was not open to the trade unions but the Company was very much more in the public eye and there is no doubt that it would have been regarded as a target by the whole trade union movement. While, under the new legislation, a defence through the courts was possible it was never a real alternative to enter a route which would lead to a long period of acrimony and pressure from all manner of sources. And this, at the critical start-up period, would detract from the essential task of building high quality motor cars with the development of innovative and constructive relationships.

As important as this however was where we would end up. In both Companies we wished to develop, in addition to harmonious relations, flexibility and common terms and conditions of employment. All of this pointed to one trade union. The view in both Continental and Nissan was that if we sought to be non-union we could end up in a multi-union situation. Recognition claims would come from a variety of trade unions – skilled and unskilled, engineering, supervisory and administrative. There would then have rapidly developed a situation which would be difficult to control. Thus, attempting to be non-union would not only dissipate management energies but could end up in a situation in which the company was not master of its own destiny.

Therefore on a rational basis both Continental and Nissan made the decision to recognise trade unionism. But in both cases there were many who simply felt it was the right thing to do – that people have the right to join a union, that the company should recognise the union and people should join the union which represents them. The issue of principle is simple.

The next decision was one union or multi-union. Much of the thinking on this developed through the union non-union analysis. We were aiming for unity of purpose; for single status and for complete flexibility. Different unions have different interests – skilled or unskilled, white-collar or blue-collar and while they might indicate that they are prepared to sit down together there are enough examples in virtually every manufacturing company in the UK to make it absolutely certain that such unity would have but a short life, Sooner or later something would happen and one group would claim that its differential had been eroded or that the less skilled had trespassed too far on the more skilled person's work, or vice versa, and the unity which in principle was great, in practice would dissolve in mutual recriminations.

We also realised that if we recognised two unions the logical base for single unionism would be eroded. If we accepted that there could be one union for the skilled and one union for the semi-skilled why could there not be another for the clerks, another for the supervisors and another for the engineers? Again this would mitigate against what we were trying to achieve and while not an immediate disaster would at some time in the future result in a tendency at best to pull apart and at worst to break the unity that was our target.

Having concluded therefore that we were interested in having only one trade union we had to determine which members of the staff should be entitled to be represented by that union. This question has had to be faced by many organisations that have opted for 'single union – single status' and generally the answer has been different to the Continental and Nissan conclusion, most having opted for a union agreement that covers only manual workers or at most takes in also the clerical staff.

Continental determined that the agreement with the trade union would cover all levels up to Electrical Engineer and Mechanical Engineer. This incorporated Janitors, Clerks, Maintainers, Supervisors, Personnel officers and Shift Managers. The logic of this was simple. If Continental was to have genuine single status the employment package would be common to all and if it were to have one trade union then that union would negotiate that package on behalf of all. Conversely, if it had been decided that the eventually selected trade union would represent only manual workers there would forever be the risk that the non-represented sections would take the view that a particular negotiation or agreement did not adequately reflect their views. They would in effect be disenfranchised and as a result there would be pressure from that group to establish another body which would more properly represent its interests. Were that to happen, Continental was concerned that the carefully constructed single status agreement would begin to fray at the edges and in a particularly serious situation there would be potential for it pulling apart.

From this it is apparent that Nissan does not have a closed shop – neither does Continental – but clearly between the establishment of the two companies the political atmosphere changed. Few practising industrial relations managers in the 1970s had philosophical objections to the closed shop. The argument was that people *were* going to become members of a trade union which would negotiate terms and conditions of employment on behalf of all staff. It was better if the union negotiators could genuinely represent all employees in these negotiations and there was an instinctive prejudice against 'free riders'. Additionally most practising industrial relations managers have come across the active non-unionist who takes a delight in seeking to upset the local union hierarchy, and in the process creates significant union-management relationship problems particularly when it reaches the point when a local trade union group determines that it will not work with the individual. This puts the local management in a difficult position as legally no account can be taken of employee pressure when determining whether or not to dismiss an employee and even if the management decides to move the individual to another position the possibility of constructive dismissal now looms.

In summary the view of many practising industrial relations managers in the 1970s (and probably still held by many now) was that 'if we're going to have most employees in the union we would prefer to have all of them in'.

However with the policy decision that Continental would not have a closed shop the company made no mention of the issue anywhere in the Agreement which stated on this question in Paragraph 1(d) 'The Company recognises the right of its employees to belong to the Union and of the Union to represent its members' interests'. However the agreement also provided for 'check off' (the deduction of trade union subscriptions from salary and the subsequent remission of these subscriptions by the Company to the Union). The relevant clause in the 'check off' agreement stated 'Deduction of membership subscriptions will become a condition of employment for all members of the Union.' Between 1979 and 1985 however there occurred a number of significant political and economic changes which had the combined effect of making it not only more difficult to establish a closed shop but, perhaps significantly more important, establishing the atmosphere in which a closed shop became socially less acceptable. This change has had an effect not only on management but on trade unions. Indeed there now appears to be a recognition that in an existing non-union situation, whether it be a greenfield site or otherwise, closed shops are a practical impossibility. This does not mean that where they already exist they cannot be maintained (indeed the evidence is that in those companies in which there have been ballots on maintaining an existing closed shop the vote has gone in favour of continuation) but that where they do not exist the trade union will to newly establish them is no longer there. There is now a recognition that trade unions, like virtually all other organisations have to *earn* membership not *require* it.

This change in atmosphere was clearly reflected in the agreement Nissan eventually reached with the AEU which stated, as for Continental, 'The Company recognises the right of its employees to belong to the Union and of the Union to represent its members' but also added in a later paragraph 'The Company will encourage its employees to join the Union and to take an active part in Union activities' and then 'An employee who chooses not to be a member of the Union will receive no discrimination, either favourable or unfavourable, by the Company or the Union.'

To most companies which talk in their agreements about encouraging Union membership the phrase is just so many words. But Nissan has actively encouraged membership both directly and by giving the Union officials full access to new hires. While membership has initially not exceeded 25 per cent both the company and the AEU are convinced that as the company rapidly expands membership levels will grow.

The actual process of selecting a trade union (and the use of that phrase 'selecting a trade union' is anathema to many in the union movement, being disparagingly described by some as 'a beauty contest') was virtually identical in both Continental and Nissan. In Continental the starting-off point was some very early advice, 'Talk to every union that could conceivably have an interest in representing your employees and then make a decision as to which union best fits Continental – those not selected will respect that decision.' At that time, late 1978, this advice was received with some surprise among Continental's British executives.

However, in the industrial areas of both South and North Wales a number of companies had developed single union agreements by going down this route and provided the non-selected unions were satisfied that they had been given a fair opportunity of laying claim to negotiating rights then, while they might not like the company's decision they would accept it. Again it was emphasised to us that it would be *the company's* decision. This also met with some initial incredulity. However, accepting that the advice was based on experience which had proved in the past to be successful, Continental wisely decided to accept it and also to conduct such discussions under the auspices of the Welsh TUC.

The question remained as to which unions should be considered. Some had approached Continental – the Transport and General Workers Union and the Iron and Steel Trades Confederation, others had a traditional role in the industry – the National Graphical Association and, in the North Wales area, the Amalgamated Union of Engineering Workers and General and Municipal Workers could not be ignored. But here Continental, and later Nissan, were faced with another fundamental question. Requiring one trade union, could a union which traditionally represents manual workers also represent their supervisors, administrative personnel and engineers? Most companies who have gone down the single union route have opted out of this question either by also recognising the 'staff' section of the appropriate manual union to represent the traditional 'staff' categories or by simply having the traditional staff categories not represented at all. Continental and Nissan considered both alternatives but the logic of single status points to one Union and even if, as in the case of the TGWU in North Wales, the same Regional Official covered both the manual and staff sections, separate sections of the same union would mitigate against the unity that was in the process of being created and could eventually lead to a split. Those companies that have gone down the non-representation road have made what they consider to be the right decision but they tend to be in the frontier technology sector where the nature of the staff they employ makes it less likely that they will wish to join a trade union anyway. Manufacturing of the type in which Continental and Nissan are involved is an entirely different situation.

Thus the decision was made that one union actually means one union and not separate sections of one union. During the subsequent discussions with the various trade unions which wished to represent Continental's employees this issue was explored in some depth and the conclusion was fundamental to the future of the company. All the unions indicated that while they had a traditional manual base they were perfectly capable of representing all categories of employee.

The concept of 'single status – single union' was new to virtually all trade union officials. Most have had experience of some aspect of the package but none had taken it to the length that Continental was proposing. However the logic of the argument was inescapable and it was emphasised that an attempt was being made to break the mould – not only were we talking about a different type of agreement between the company and the union but also we discussed openly and frankly our developing management philosophy. The trade union officials of every union and in both localities found this exciting and wanted to be part of it. Without exception they recognised the validity of the arguments and supported the concept of 'single union – single status'.

A decision on which union is not made solely on the attitude of the officials to the draft agreement. Before arriving at the meetings both trade unions and management are sensible if they do their homework, and management investigates the background of the unions, both local and national and make an assessment of the so called 'comfort' factor which ranks very highly in the decision-making process. However good the objective evidence may be on paper, if the assessment does not 'feel' right the decision may go another way. Particularly in matters relating to industrial relations so much depends on the 'gut feel' of the negotiators which, while it may not be possible to express it in words, so often is the reason for decisions being made.

Most of the factors taken into account in making the Union decisions were common to both Continental and Nissan. The National politics of the Union is a factor – is it on the left, right or centre? There is no doubt that at the time of both the Continental and Nissan decisions the TGWU was regarded as the most left wing of the main contenders. Under the leadership of Moss Evans and his policy of passing authority to the branches (and hence to the activists) the Union had moved to the left. The AEU and GMB are both regarded as right-inclined trade unions, but in no case did the national politics of the trade unions seriously enter into the decision making process. Much more important when looking at the political spectrum is the attitude of the regions in which the company will be operating.

None of the main unions either in North Wales or North-east could be described as being on the far left of union politics. The experience of the last few years, particularly in the development areas where the traditional industries have run down to a point of almost non-existence, has resulted in the development of an attitude among trade union officials that they must do everything possible to asist in attracting industry and commerce to their Regions. While they might fight to preserve threatened jobs they work hard and understand the new thinking introduced by companies like Continental and Nissan. This does not mean that the officials do not negotiate to secure a good deal for their members but they all clearly recognise where the priorities lie.

In both Continental and Nissan a comprehensive study was undertaken of industrial relations practices in the areas in which the Companies were to start their operations. This included discussions with various other companies, the names of many having been provided by the Unions themselves as being organisations with which they bargained and had good relation-ships. From this process it emerged in North Wales that the TGWU was the front runner for, surprisingly, it came out that the TGWU in the area had, through its Regional Secretary, Jim Morris, led the way in developing single union agreements with a number of organisations, and that all sections of the manual workforce were prepared to join the TGWU. Gradually then during the investigation process the company concluded that the best decision was to recognise the TGWU as being the union to have sole bargaining rights on behalf of Continental employees. The aspect of people being willing to join the selected union was very important. What Continental did not want was a situation in which it recognised the TGWU but significant proportions of its staff refused to join. At the time it was felt that while this might be the case in other parts of the country it was not so in North Wales – and this view proved to be correct. Since then there have been no significant pressures to change that decision and the TGWU continues to give full and fair representation to all groups.

The situation in Nissan was complicated by the media interest in the union question and the fact that there were three strong front runners in the North-east. The largest union in the North-east is the GMB whose Regional Secretary Tom Burlison is also Chairman of the Northern TUC. As expected the GMB is particularly strong in the Public Services and Shipyards and has some single union or sole bargaining rights deals with North-eastern companies.

The TGWU is strong in transport and the docks and is represented in almost all companies in the area. Again the TGWU has a number of single union deals in the North-east. The AEU also has single union deals with a number of companies and is strong in the engineering sector, shipbuilding, and represents most mechanical craftsmen in virtually all companies. This, Nissan found, was a very significant point and one in which the North-east could be said to differ from North Wales. In those companies where the TGWU or GMB had sole bargaining rights the craftsmen have generally remained as members of the AEU. In those companies where the AEU has sole bargaining rights the general workers have been prepared to join that union, not insisting on retaining the general workers' union membership. Thus Nissan had in the North-east a situation which Continental expected in North Wales but did not find, that the craftsmen were less prepared to join a union they perceived to be 'general' than the general workers were to join a union which they perceived to be 'skilled'. 'Perceived to be' are the operative words for the strict divisions between skilled and general unions no longer exist – both are able to and do recruit almost anybody who is prepared to join.

In the end however the Nissan decision to recognise the AEU came not from any assessment of the political tendencies of the unions, the numerical strength in the region or who would give us the best deal but from our judgement as to which Union our employees were most likely to join. We believed that with a single union more of our employees across the spectrum of occupations would join the AEU then the TGWU or GMB. A number of commentators have suggested other motives, laying particular emphasis on the supposed national moderation of the AEU as opposed to the TGWU. But all such tendencies are transitory and to base a decision on such a factor would have lead us down the wrong path. There simply was no ulterior motive in the Nissan decision.

Other companies have approached the situation differently. Inmos in seeking a Union to represent its office, technician and operative staff surveyed its employees and found 53 per cent in favour of one union, 34 per cent wanting no union and 5 per cent a variety. Under the auspices of the Welsh TUC Inmos met with a number of Unions before deciding on the EETPU. Findus, which recognised a multiplicity of unions at its Humberside plants opted for the AEU and the GMB when opening a new plant at Long Benton, north of Newcastle. Findus however in recognising that more than one union could create difficulties included in its Agreement a statement that 'it is the intention of all parties that this agreement will not create divisions or demarcation between different groups of employees'. It also provided for representation on a group rather than union basis and that 'Meetings convened to discuss the affairs of only one union group will not be recognised by the company'.

Most of the Japanese companies in the electronics sector have opted for single union deals – mainly with the EETPU although a pioneer, Sony in South Wales, reached agreement with the AEU. The Anglo-Canadian Optical Fibres chose the white-collar section of the EETPU – EESA, the Electrical and Engineering Staff Association – following consultation at the end of 1982 with those employees who had by then joined the company. Toshiba's agreement with the EETPU covers both production personnel and clerical staff and while it is the most aggressive in pushing single unionism the EETPU is not alone for, given the right circumstances, all unions would be happy to sign single union or sole bargaining rights deals.

In a more traditional area, the Iron and Steel Trades Confederation signed a single union deal with United Merchant Bar (a newly formed joint venture between Coparo Industries and British Steel Corporation) in early 1986. Covering administrative, production and maintenance staff, the deal was similar to that offered by the AEU and EETPU and includes many aspects – including flexibility and pendulum arbitration common to such packages.

Often regarded as being one of the unions most critical of single union deals, the TGWU signed such an agreement with Short Brothers, the Belfast-based aerospace manufacturers, in November 1985. The deal gave the TGWU negotiating rights for all employees up to management level at Short's new plant on the site of the De Lorean car factory. Under the terms of the agreement only the TGWU will have negotiating rights although it is accepted that some employees may wish to join another union 'acceptable to the Union and the Company'. It is not clear what constitutes 'acceptable'.

Without doubt however the most contentious of the single union deals has been at Hitachi where following that company's total takeover from its previous 50–50 deal with GEC it reached a single union agreement with the EETPU thus displacing the AEU, UCATT, APEX and ASTMS. Prompted as much as anything by the EETPU–Hitachi situation the TUC amended its Disputes Principles and Procedures in December 1985. Previously the signing of sole negotiating rights or membership agreements was acceptable provided the union involved took account of the position of other unions. The new section states, however, that

> When making sole negotiating rights or union membership agreements or arrangements, affiliated unions must have regard to the interests of other unions which may be affected and should consider their position in the drafting of such agreements. No union shall enter into a sole negotiating agreement, union membership agreement or any other form of agreement in any circumstances including a takeover or change of ownership or some other reason where another union(s) would be deprived of their existing rights of recognition except by prior consultation and agreement of the other union(s) concerned.

This was further reinforced following the EETPU's activities at

News International's Wapping plant in early 1986 when in a specific directive to the EETPU the General Council added

> Where agreement cannot be reached through consultation between the Unions concerned the issue will be referred to the TUC for advice and conciliation and if necessary a Disputes Committee adjudication.

Not only does this mean no more Hitachis but virtually limits future single union deals to greenfield sites unless agreement can be reached with the potential displaced unions.

It is somewhat ironic that, although initiated by ASTMS, a party to one of the first complaints under this new procedure was the EETPU, following the takeover by Norsk Hydro of the Fisons plant at Immingham, Humberside. Previously Fisons had recognised five trade unions (ASTMS, EETPU, TGWU, AEU and UCATT) but the new owners proposed a single-union deal. While going through the procedural discussions the company also made the decision to ballot employees directly, and as a result two-thirds voted in favour of a single union, the TGWU. Because the process had not been initiated by the unions and the TGWU had not sought a single union deal it was not criticised by the TUC. Although the single-union agreement was implemented by Norsk Hydro and was effectively in operation the TGWU had still not signed it by mid-1987.

In his study of these events Ian Linn stated that the site unions were 'comprehensively outflanked by the company' and that unless unions are as 'flexible as management in their tactics then companies will be successful in individualising the union members' choice'.[2] The new TUC policy does have clear implications for managements in existing organisations seeking to change to single union deals. Sun Alliance Insurance Group was prepared to sign a single union deal with ASTMS excluding the Banking Insurance and Finance Union. The TUC Disputes Committee in May 1986 in its first decision under the new policy ruled that ASTMS could not sign such an agreement without BIFU's prior agreement. It required them to 'work in harmony' and gave them eight weeks to agree a basis for joint recognition. By September 1986 when the issue had still not been resolved, the TUC Disputes Committee instructed ASTMS not to proceed as the sole union but meet management with BIFU to press for joint recognition. ASTMS' failure to respond led to the TUC General

Council voting in December 1986 to begin formal disciplinary proceedings against it and it was at this point that ASTMS backed down and agreed to joint representation. A clear victory for the TUC! The fact that Unions may now feel obliged to abide by the TUC's new guidelines on single union deals does not of course obligate the company involved if it is determined to stick with one trade union. Hitachi which, because of its rejection of previously established unions was more instrumental than most in bringing about the new policy, has clearly indicated that it was not affected by the TUC rules. In the first case which could have given rise to another union being involved, a member of UCATT who was dismissed was not allowed to be represented by his own union.

Yuasa Battery in Ebbw Vale, South Wales, has also found itself caught in a recognition dispute between the TGWU and EETPU. Following inter-union wrangling about recruitment methods the company signed a single-union deal with the EETPU in June 1986. As the result of a complaint to the TUC Disputes Committee the EETPU was instructed to withdraw from its deal and cease meeting the company. Both unions were directed not to approach Yuasa for recognition for eight weeks but both subsequently claimed that the other had breached this requirement. The TUC stipulated that after the eight-week period both could seek joint recognition but it then stated that *if the company refused joint recognition but would be prepared to deal with one union* those employees who were in the non-recognised union should be allowed to retain their membership. This ruling appears to recognise that if an employer wishes to ignore it then there is little that can be done – and Yuasa subsequently re-signed with the EETPU!

Both Continental and Nissan recognised and encouraged trade union membership but both felt that such membership should not be a barrier to good open communication between the company and its staff. So often in British industry there has developed the practice that management is barely able to talk to employees – that is the shop steward's right. Thus both Agreements specifically provide for open communication – 'This Agreement complements the right of the Company to communicate directly with its employees' (Continental) and 'both parties are agreed on the need ... to maintain open and direct communication with all employees on matters of mutual interest and concern' (Nissan). This was combined with the other General Principles of the Nissan–AEU Agreement ('to promote and maintain mutual trust and cooperation between the Company, its employees and the Union ... to recognise that all employees at whatever level have a valued part to play in the success of the Company ... to seek actively the contributions of all employees in furtherance of these goals') to lay the foundations of the open communicative style of management that Nissan wished to adopt.

However, while placing the emphasis for establishing good relationships firmly with line management, Nissan and the AEU were agreed that a more formal body was needed. Virtually all large companies have such a body, variously called Joint Works Committee, Works Council, Consultative Committee and so on. Most have several, each representing different sections of the workforce. The Nissan model was borrowed from Inmos and enjoys the same title – the Company Council.

It was the intention of both Nissan and the AEU that if all employees were to be covered by the Agreement with common terms and conditions of employment there needed to be only one such body. On this would sit representatives of all employees – Manufacturing Staff, Technicians, their Supervisors, Engineers, Purchasing staff, Accountants, and so on. What unites people because they are all Nissan staff is stronger than what divides them because one is a Supervisor and the other is supervised.

Under its constitution the Company Council is charged with 'promoting effective communication and harmonious relations between the Company, its employees and the Union'. It recognised that 'all concerned have a mutual interest in ensuring the prosperity of the Company and thus promoting the prosperity and security of all employees'. Real security comes not from a long term contract but from working for a vigorous, successful enterprise. It is rare indeed in the UK for the constitution of any Works Committee to even mention joint responsibility for the well being of the Company. They are usually more concerned with providing a forum to perpetuate the adversarial nature of British industrial relations!

The Nissan Company Council has three main roles – it is a consultative forum, it is the final stage of the in-house grievance procedure and, at entirely separate meetings from the regular quarterly sessions, it is responsible for negotiating salaries and conditions. Starting in late 1985 on an interim basis the Council successfully negotiated the salary increase effective from 1 January 1986 and the salary structure that went with it. All representatives did act together and, while it was recognised that there was much to learn, it actually worked. Representatives of all departments and occupations were able to agree a package which was accepted by all employees and subsequently was ratified by the full time official of the AEU under whose auspices negotiations take place. In late 1986 the Council concluded a two year salary deal effective from January 1987.

Under its constitution the Company Council is required to report twice yearly to all employees. The first such report in March 1987 was in written form but in conjunction with this presentation the company decided that all Directors would give a report of the activities of their departments. Thus all employees gathered together and for 30 minutes received a series of very short presentations aimed at explaining every aspect of the company's business. The most important element of such sessions is, however, the question period. In many companies the comments are of the type 'It's all right you talking about investing millions of pounds but I've been trying to get a window mended for six months and nobody seems interested!' Significantly the questions at the Nissan presentations have been at the same level as the information given. This can be interpreted as meaning both that the workforce has a high level of sophistication and that the supervisors are able to handle all the irritating issues before they become major problems that need a public airing.

It is not a requirement that employees elected to the Company Council be members of the union – but some are. And as the company develops the proportion is likely to grow. It remains important that employees feel that they are properly represented both individually and collectively and that the union *as* the union also has an important role with the union official having a right of access to both the company and employees. It should be remembered however that in the vast majority of small companies, negotiations are settled in-house without direct involvement of the union officials. Only if there is in-house failure to agree do they turn for outside help.

But what happens when in-house agreement cannot be reached? ... Do 'no strike' agreements really exist?

I don't care if you criticise us, agree with us or disagree with us, just mention us, that is all we ask – *David Owen, Leader of the SDP.*

There is no such thing as a no strike agreement – *Peter Wickens, Personnel Director, Nissan Motor Manufacturing (UK) Ltd*

People don't know where to put their hands when they're guiding you. They sometimes touch bare flesh – *Diana, Princess of Wales.*[3]

Sandwiched between the Leader of the Social Democratic Party and the Princess of Wales in The *Observer*'s Quotations of the Week was the phrase uttered by both Nissan and the AEU at the Press Conference announcing the signing of the single union agreement. Anticipating the direction of media interest the Company's press statement included the comment 'The Agreement also provides that during the course of such negotiations, conciliation or arbitration there will be no industrial action but neither Nissan nor the AEU see this as a 'no-strike agreement'. Reference to arbitration is not 100 per cent automatic but what we are attempting to do is to eliminate the *need* for industrial action'.

In 1979 at the time the Continental–TGWU agreement was being prepared the phrase 'no strike deal' was hardly in common usage. The EETPU deals with various Japanese electronics companies had barely hit the headlines. However, this is not to say that no strike deals have not existed previously. The Ford Motor Company multi-union procedure agreement states

> The Parties agree that, at each stage of the procedure set out in this Agreement, every attempt will be made to resolve the issues raised and that until such procedure is carried through there shall be no stoppage of work or other unconstitutional action.

More recently the National Union of Seamen agreed in February 1986 a procedure to operate within the Royal Fleet Auxiliary that both parties believe will eliminate the need for strikes – although no one is prepared to call it a 'no strike' deal. The 'Undertaking on limitation of industrial action' commits the parties

> to refrain from stoppages of work, lockouts or any other form of industrial action until procedures for settling points of differences have been exhausted.

In this it is little different to probably thousands of agreements operational in British industry (although the RFA–NUS deal does provide for the RFA to apply to the NUS for exemption from general strike action) which broadly can be categorised as stating 'No industrial action while an issue is in procedure'.

Such agreements do not even date from the last twenty years. One, dated 26 February 1935, is between the major railway companies and the NUR, ASLEF and the Railway Clerks' Association. Paragraph 18 of the Memorandum of Agreement states 'In no circumstances shall there be any withdrawal of labour or any attempt on the part of employees to hamper the proper working of the Railway, until any matter in dispute has been submitted through the proper channels to the Higher Management, or if such matter is within the scope of the Machinery of Negotiation, until the provisions thereof have been fully utilised'. In traditional industrial relations little changes!

A similar device was developed at Continental Can Company which stated under the General Principles of the Agreement with the TGWU 'both parties are agreed on the need to ... avoid any action that interrupts the continuity of production and employment'. And in the section dealing with negotiations, 'During the course of such negotiations there will be no industrial action'. This was virtually repeated at the end of the grievance procedure 'There will be no industrial action of any kind while an issue is in Procedure and for a further five working days following completion of the Procedure unless authorised by the Union Executive'.

The Electricians' Union first came to the fore in taking such agreements a step further in the 1960s when in an attempt to bring some sort of order into the electrical contracting industry – which in 1962 lost some 37 000 man days through industrial action – they agreed with the Electrical Contractors' Association a procedure which provided for Regional and National level boards to investigate and resolve matters referred to them within ten working days. Under the terms of this Agreement 'no disputes panel or appeals panel will meet on any grievance unless those concerned are working normally'. While not entirely due to the Agreement it is not insignificant that 1962's 37 000 man days lost had dropped to 500 by 1983.

Being able to demonstrate a record of achievement and of course being, in skill terms, the appropriate union, it is not surprising that the EETPU was attractive to the Japanese electronics companies beginning to establish themselves in the UK in the late 1970s and early 1980s. With their requirements for relationships similar to those experienced at home, combined with a union seeking to extend its influence in one of the few growth areas of the British economy the growth of agreements between the Japanese and the EETPU was both rapid and revolutionary. While covering very much more than the much publicised procedure agreements (now totalling around 20) a typical paragraph in this area is contained in the 1981 deal with Toshiba

> both the Company and the Union recognise this approach provides for the resolution of conflicts of interest between the Company and its employees through consultation, negotiation and arbitration rather than the traditional processes of industrial action .... If the matter is not resolved a joint reference shall be made to an independent arbitrator .... The terms of reference of the arbitrator will be to find in favour of either the Company or the trade union. A compromise solution shall not be recommended. Both parties agree to abide by the decision of the arbitrator.

Sanyo and the EETPU agreed in June 1982 that

> The Company and the Union undertake to follow the procedure agreed and to recognise this agreement provides adequate and speedy procedures for the discussion of company related affairs and the resolution of problems and as such precludes the necessity for recourse to any form of industrial action by either the Company, the union or the employees.

and then on arbitration

> In the event that the Company and the union shall be unable ultimately to resolve between themselves any discussions or disputes they may jointly agree to appoint an arbitrator ... the arbitrator will decide in favour of one party. The decision will be final and binding and will represent the final solution to the issue.

The Toshiba and Sanyo agreements provide for automatic reference to arbitration. A variation on the theme was developed by Control Data (now Xidex Corporation) and the EETPU in January 1984.

The purpose of the negotiating procedure is to establish methods of resolving problems to the agreement of all parties concerned without recourse to any form of action which would be detrimental to the business and employment prospects.

Allowing for three internal forums, the in house procedure provides for secret ballots at the end of both the second (local) forum and the third (executive) forum before the matter is referred outside the company for conciliation (not, it should be noted, arbitration).

At this level ACAS will be invited to act as conciliators to bring both parties to agreement. A period not exceeding 30 days will be allowed for this process to be completed and it is incumbent on all parties involved to resolve the matter finally.

The Control Data procedure concludes by stating 'A fundamental understanding is that during any phase of this new procedure all normal working practices are observed and maintained.'

The significant point about these deals is not that they are designed to prevent disputes while an issue is in procedure – as we have seen many agreements include such provisions – but that once the in-house procedure is exhausted they require automatic reference to an outside body – normally ACAS – to resolve the issue, frequently on a pendulum basis. Like the phrase 'no strike', 'pendulum arbitration' is an often misunderstood term which does not mean the arbitrator decides alternately in favour of the Company and the union but on each occasion decides fully in favour of one party or the other – no compromise – with both parties committed in advance to accept the decision. Thus they can be more accurately described as 'disputes procedures with built-in resolution'. ACAS prefers the term 'new style' agreements and also uses 'straight choice' as opposed to 'pendulum' arbitration.

Other early agreements were concentrated in the electronics industry eg Inmos, Optical Fibres and AB Electronics. But the net is now spreading. NEK, a Norwegian cable manufacturer based a few miles from Nissan, has a compulsory arbitration agreement with the GMB. Sometimes the 'no strike' element may not be specific. The Scottish and Newcastle Breweries deal with the TGWU states that 'no meetings to negotiate a settlement can take place unless normal working is being carried out'. However, prior to the Nissan agreement it is true that employees covered by 'no strike' agreements generally were of a type less likely than most to go on strike anyway. Typically, highly qualified graduates and young female light assembly workers, their level of militancy is normally low and even without a 'no strike' agreement it would seem unlikely that such companies would be plagued by the 'British disease' which so frightens potential inward investors.

Such agreements form however only one part of the story, for those companies which have sought this route combine the 'no strike element' with many other innovative practices. Reviewing four of the early agreements (Toshiba, Optical Fibres, Inmos and Control Data). *Industrial Relations Review and Report*[4] concluded that they provide

> an inexhaustible disputes procedure accompanied by a wide range of harmonisation, flexibility and participation measures – together these arrangements are designed to create a consensual atmosphere in which industrial action becomes unnecessary – the 'no strike' clause which may not be specific can be seen as a formalisation of the whole approach

This point has been frequently emphasised by the EETPU who deny accusations that they are selling out hard won rights.[5] Their approach is to achieve a package deal which includes single status, training and retraining and the provision of a high level of information. They will argue that there is no such thing as a 'no strike' agreement but believe that traditional trade union behaviour is outdated.

Although not fully supporting the EETPU view, the General Secretary of the TUC Norman Willis when speaking at the IPM Annual Conference in Harrogate (October 1986) clearly recognised that the desire to strike was no longer to the forefront of employee thinking. 'I have no doubt that, increasingly, members will be looking to their unions to provide progress without strikes and without pickets – quite simply, with the minimum of hassle, especially self-induced hassle'. And then equally significantly 'Unions relate to their members. There can be no doubt that unions will ignore at their peril questions about how they are perceived by their members'.

The EETPU is (apart from the Royal College of Nursing which is a special case) the only union which has fully embraced the

'inexhaustable procedure' concept. Indeed, in the very week that
Nissan signed its deal with the AEU, the union's Executive
Committee, meeting in Eastbourne, had before it six resolutions
condemning such arrangements which are seen by many trade
unionists as giving away one of the most fundamental rights –
the right to strike. However in defence of its position the EETPU
would say that not only do such agreements not give away the
right to strike (although with the inexhaustible disputes procedure it is difficult to see how such strikes could be constitutional)
but also that they deal with the formal procedural situation only.
They do not and cannot stop the 'wild cat' strikes brought about
by militant, unofficial, action on the shop floor which according
to various sources comprise more than 90 per cent of industrial
action.

What is there then to suggest that these new style agreements
are going to work any better than the traditional agreements? We
have already seen that one element – 'built in resolution' is but
one factor in a total package including not only flexibility and
harmonisation but also a management approach which seeks to
resolve issues within the procedure rather than by adopting an
adversarial style. In addition to this is the provision for
pendulum arbitration.

Traditionally arbitration has meant that following a failure to
agree at Company level and possibly in the middle of a dispute
one or both sides refers the issue, in whole or part, to an
arbitrator and in so doing they may or may not agree in advance
to accept the decision. Additionally, ACAS stands for Advisory,
Conciliation and Arbitration Service and both sides may or may
not take advantage of the Conciliation part of the service –
although generally ACAS would prefer conciliation before
arbitration.

However many industrial relations practitioners in the UK (on
both sides) are reluctant to go to arbitration, not wishing an
outsider to determine the solution. Reference to arbitration is
believed to result, if not in compromise, at least in an addition to
the last offer and a frequently spoken view is 'If I'm prepared to
give more I can do it myself without anyone's help. If I'm not
prepared to, then I will fight it out!' This attitude may work if the
Agreement requires both sides to agree to a reference to
arbitration but some, e.g. British Gas, allow for unilateral reference.
Frequent use of unilateral arbitration can result in the Company

'keeping something up its sleeve' and the unions, knowing this, are more likely to believe they will get something additional by pursuing arbitration. Thus, as happened with British Gas in the early 1980s, a pattern can develop which eventually is of little benefit to anyone. Reference to arbitration whether by both sides or unilaterally can only be of value if it is used sparingly.

Traditional style arbitration often results in compromise (though there is little hard evidence of arbitrators splitting the difference) because the positions of the parties are wide apart. The theory of pendulum arbitration is, however, that by requiring the arbitrator to decide wholly in favour of one side then both sides arrive at a position which no arbitrator would consider unreasonable and thus decide against. An extension of this is that if both sides adopt 'reasonable' positions they will be able to resolve the matter without recourse to an outside agency. In its simplest terms this could mean that if, in that taboo phrase, the 'going rate' was six per cent, traditional bargaining would result in a final claim of eight per cent and final offer of four per cent. Bargaining which could lead to pendulum arbitration could however result in figures of 6.5 per cent and 5.6 per cent – a not unbridgeable gap.

Unfortunately life in practice is not always like the theory. Claims and offers are not usually restricted to a movement on basic pay but include reference to other aspects of the employment package – holiday entitlement, hours of work, shift premia, pensions, and so on. While the employer may be willing to agree six per cent plus two additional days holiday and an increase in bonus payments he may not be prepared to give the same balance if the basic pay award is increased. Thus it is possible for the arbitrator to be presented not with a simple pay claim but a complex package, with many variables depending on the nature of the claim and offer. As a result it is not inconceivable that the arbitrator could drift back into the compromising balancing act to which he is more naturally suited. This has in fact happened in the United States where arbitrators faced with a complex package of claim and offer have ruled on each part of the package separately ending up with a balanced total award. Not in line with the overall philosophy, this practice has caused Sir John Wood, Chairman of the Central Arbitration Committee to state 'If this modification finds favour it has to be asked whether the process has not in effect come full circle'.[6]

This potential difficulty is well recognised by the Central Arbitration Committee which has been somewhat critical of the type of procedure ending in compulsory pendulum arbitration. Recognising that it is likely to be the complex issues that fail to be resolved the CAC is a little wary of being faced with finding wholly in favour of one side or the other. 'In dealing with a complex multi-element claim and offer, too, with each side offering convincing arguments in some areas, the right answer may be to award differentially: i.e. for the employer on some aspects and the union on others'. This of course is ruled out by 'simple' pendulum arbitration. Further the CAC Report recognises that the processes leading to pendulum arbitration are as much about changing the structure of bargaining as about resolving in-house failures to agree. 'But what' asks the CAC, 'if this basic premise is not met and the arbitrators are presented with a difficult task in which the parties remain far apart and which can only be solved by a choice between two extremes?'[7]

It was against this background of change and debate that Nissan met and discussed with the trade unions. The company was clear as to its intentions and objectives and felt it important that everyone understood that the company was not trying to usurp the traditional role of trade unions. While we would have been happy to have what could be described as a 100 per cent cast iron guarantee of no industrial action it was, we felt, more important to achieve an agreement which could be honoured by all concerned than one which gave everything but which might collapse the first time it was tested. In addition to this we felt it important that as ACAS would be involved in the procedure then the ACAS views should be taken into account. Clearly ACAS has a preference for conciliation before arbitration and, as experience has shown, will try to conciliate before arbitration even when the reference is initially concerned with the latter. In providing for conciliation it was a major concern of all parties that neither the company nor the union should 'keep something up its sleeve for conciliation' – either the company a concession it could afford or the union a claim it was willing to forgo. Such attitudes would destroy the spirit of the agreement.

The eventual wording of the Negotiations paragraph of the Agreement was particularly precise:

The Company and the Union are totally committed to resolving such negotiations within the Company Council. However in exceptional circumstances if this is not possible the outstanding matters will be referred to the Advisory Conciliation and Arbitration Service for resolution.

The key phrases in this context are 'totally committed', and 'in exceptional circumstances'. Thus both parties were agreed that they would genuinely attempt on all occasions to resolve matters in-house without reference to ACAS. Reference to ACAS on any occasion is regarded as undesirable and would be an indication that people had not worked hard enough to resolve the issues in-house. In themselves such phrases do not prevent a reference to ACAS but if such a reference is used too frequently then clearly ACAS itself might choose to draw to the attention of the parties that not only the spirit but also the letter of the Agreement was not being fully honoured.

The paragraph continues

> In the event of conciliation not producing a solution both parties may agree to arbitration. The arbitrator will be required to determine positively in favour of one side or the other. The arbitrator will be asked to take account of those aspects which are already agreed. Both parties agree to accept the decision of the arbitrator ... During the course of such negotiations, conciliation or arbitration there will be no industrial action.

Thus the intention of both the company and the AEU is that in the exceptional circumstances of non-resolution in-house there will be automatic reference to ACAS for conciliation. Appreciating that the subject of the reference might be complex and that the two parties might simply need their collective heads knocking together for something sensible to fall out it was felt that conciliation was the best method of achieving this. At the very least conciliation would give ACAS a better understanding of the issues involved and help clarify those aspects which need to go through to arbitration. It might even help establish a balance of claims and offers so that a complex package claim can be more effectively handled. At its best, conciliation might resolve the problem by a third party looking at the issues in a way that was not obvious to the committed parties. What would be a failure, however, would be the company 'finding' another one per cent at the conciliation stage. This would lead to virtual automatic future reference to conciliation particularly if employees perceived that they had nothing to lose and possibly something to gain – especially if precluded by the Agreement from taking industrial action at this stage.

The Agreement, while also providing that reference to ACAS will be 'for resolution', implicitly recognised that this might not always be possible at the conciliation stage. The key wording here was 'In the event of conciliation not producing a solution both parties may agree to arbitration'. While, having gone through the in-house negotiations and subsequent conciliation, there would be considerable pressure on both parties to take the final step to arbitration, there is no compulsion in the Agreement for them to do so. It needs the agreement of both the company and the union to take that step to pendulum arbitration with prior commitment to accept the decision. It follows then that the Nissan–AEU procedure agreement can end after the conciliation phase. If this is the case, and it is the union that does not wish to proceed, industrial action taken at this time would be constitutional. It is in this specific as well as the general sense that the Nissan–AEU Agreement cannot be described as a 'no strike deal'.

At least to some commentators, Nissan has avoided some of the problems envisaged by the Central Arbitration Committee. An IDS report *Collective Bargaining*[8] indicated that it saw a clear distinction between the more normal compulsory arbitration and Nissan's compulsory conciliation. Nissan's approach, according to IDS, is 'unlikely to lead to the problems outlined by the CAC'.

How have these agreements worked in practice? The fact that there have been few such references and even fewer instances of industrial action demonstrates either that the procedures work well or that such procedures are established in companies which are unlikely to fail to agree anyway. However, to the surprise of many, Peter Parker, Director of the ACAS Advisory Service, reported to the 1986 conference of the Institute of Personnel Management that eleven pendulum arbitration references had been handled by ACAS in the preceding two years. Of these, eight were decided in favour of the employer and three in favour of the union. Interestingly, none of the references were from companies with single union deals and none involved Japanese companies; five different unions were involved. Again emphasising that so called 'no strike' agreements could not prevent strikes, Parker stated that the new concepts would 'reinforce the pressure for consensus and render redundant any need for resort to industrial action'.

Of the few that have been reported, one company, Bowman Webber – a mirror and glass processing company of Harlow, Essex – has experienced both a strike and pendulum arbitration. Despite the signing of a 'no strike' deal with the EETPU in January 1985 (though employees also belong to other unions) the Company did experience a strike in January 1986 following the decision to dismiss three employees during their probationary period. Lasting for about ten days and involving about one third of the company's workforce, the problem was resolved by putting two of the three back on probation and upholding the dismissal of the other. Apart from anything else the EETPU officials at the plant argued that the strike demonstrated that no strike deals really do not mean no strikes.

Bowman Webber's second experience came some three months later following a change from single to double shift working. Significantly, the actual shift change was implemented before agreement had been reached on the shift premium rate but failing in-house agreement the union's claim for a weekly shift working wage of £160.31 against the company's offer of £151.91 was referred to ACAS. Conciliation did not resolve the issue and the difference progressed to arbitration. This gap, £8.40, was larger than that anticipated by pendulum arbitration theory and presented the arbitrator, who was more used to finding a compromise, with some difficulty. Eventually, however, he decided in favour of the union (on the grounds that the union had better substantiated its case on relative shift rates in the area) the ruling was accepted by the company and payment backdated to the start of the new shift pattern. The EETPU was of course delighted with the result, presenting it as a vindication of their stand. While the company was less happy with the result, it was no doubt pleased with having got its double shift system implemented at the time it wanted without a dispute: and that is what it is about. The arbitrator indicated afterwards that he would have been happier to compromise.

Another argument to have been tested beyond the in-house negotiations is that of Control Data which, shortly after its takeover by Xidex Corporation, proposed a pay freeze. Following rejection by secret ballot the pay freeze was referred to ACAS for conciliation – the final stage in the procedure. During the conciliation process the Company made no significant change to its position and, in accordance with the procedure, agreement was reached very much on the basis of the pre-ballot position and without further reference to the employees.

The biggest test of the pendulum arbitration deals was however at Sanyo Industries of Lowestoft. Following the breakdown of its 1984/85 pay negotiations the parties were unable to agree how the pendulum process should operate. The procedure itself appears clear 'In the event that the company and the union shall be unable ultimately to resolve between themselves any discussions or disputes they may jointly agree to appoint an arbitrator ... The arbitrator will decide in favour of one party. The decision ... will be final and binding and will represent the final solution to the issue'.

Unfortunately, as is frequently the case in real life, people did not behave as theory predicted they would. Following initial negotiations and rejection by ballot of the company offer the union's final claim was for a three year deal which would apparently move Sanyo's rates to the 'industry average' compared to the company's one year offer of 6 per cent plus three weeks bonus. Thus, contrary to the theory of pendulum arbitration, the two sides had not come close to each other and indeed the nature of the claim and offer were very different. The position was then further confused for instead of reference to ACAS arbitration the EETPU proposed appointing a mediator, citing American experience where such practice is commonplace. Despite the fact that there is no mention of mediation in the Sanyo agreement the EETPU argued that in their understanding such a stage was implicit in the process. With the assistance of ACAS this issue was suitably massaged to allow the procedure to start but when the arbitrator, Professor Sid Kessler of City University arrived, to his and everyone elses's surprise he found that the nature of the union claim had totally changed. The three-year claim to bring the company in line with the industry average had evaporated and the company and Professor Kessler were faced with a standard one-year claim for 8 per cent. Quite possibly had this been the union's position at the end of the in-house negotiations Professor Kessler's journey could have been saved and this abrupt change caused to put it mildly, a certain amount of discussion about the procedure and the ethics of the union's position – no doubt fuelled by the company's view that pendulum arbitration on the original last position could have resulted in a decision in its favour while it was not so confident about the new 6 to 8 per cent spread.

As a result of the mediation debate and the changed claim, Professor Kessler's task changed from that of arbitrator to one of trying to find a way through the tangled web. In the end a 7 per cent solution emerged. Added to it were an extra two days' holiday, a reduction of one hour in the working week, three weeks bonus paid in January and a 'pre-review' increase for some 200 people. This resulted in process operators receiving 7 per cent and technicians 18 per cent. Commenting afterwards Roy Sanderson of the EETPU said that the procedure allowed the employees to achieve more than they would have done had the union attempted to bring them out on strike 'I know that they were in no mood for industrial action and that they would not have got the increase they wanted if they had done. Thanks to the agreement they achieved an extra one per cent'.

The solution to the specific issue did not however resolve the different interpretations of the procedure – management still feeling that the original basis of the agreement was valid and the union arguing that before actually proceeding to arbitrate the arbitrator should attempt mediation (broadly in line with the ACAS preference). In May 1985 the opposing views were put to the workforce and management's view was endorsed by a two to one majority in a secret ballot. As a result Sanyo drew up a Code of Practice subsequently endorsed by the EETPU which includes the following phrases

Clear communication between the parties is essential to prevent misunderstanding and ambiguity. To this end the parties will, at all stages of the procedure and before moving from one stage to the next, communicate in writing to each other their proposals ... At the final stage of the Joint Negotiating Council the parties will attempt to resolve by negotiation any remaining differences to the point where the union will recommend to members acceptance of the proposals and hold a ballot of union members.

What of the future? Such deals are still so exceptional that almost each one is to be remarked on. Most have been on greenfield sites with a workforce not generally prone to disruptive action. The Nissan agreement itself has worked its way through the first two sets of pay negotiations and no grievances had by July 1987 found their way into the procedure. But this is more due to the overall management of the company than the procedure agreement. Maybe the most significant development has been at Eaton Ltd (axle manufacturers), a few miles from Nissan in County Durham. Against the advice of the AEU District Secretary the plant officials signed a far-reaching agreement in Spring 1986 which covered major changes in labour flexibility, pay structure, harmonisation and a 'no strike' provision. The agreement emphasises in-house resolution of problems but then continues

> However if a situation cannot be resolved the next stage of procedure which must take place within two normal working days ... is informal conciliation or arbitration by ACAS. There shall be no stoppage of work either of a partial or general character such as a strike, lock out, go slow, work to rule, restriction of movement of material and its working, an overtime ban or restriction of any kind by either party.

The significant point is that American-owned Eaton Ltd is not in a greenfield, is not in electronics and does not employ large numbers of graduates and young females on light assembly work. It is in fact in the mainstream of British manufacturing and has suffered all the problems associated with that – including low productivity, demarcation, redundancy and disputes. Prompted as almost always by a crisis situation a new management made the decision to tackle all problems at once and as *Industrial Relations Review and Report* stated, their solution 'represents a significant stage in the process of transferring lessons from the new to the old'.[9]

When such ambitions reach Fleet Street we must be making progress. Putting aside the highly publicised activities of Eddie Shah, Rupert Murdoch and Robert Maxwell, the *Financial Times* in February 1986 proposed a package to its SOGAT '82 clerical workers stating 'We need an orderly means of resolving collective disputes to everyone's satisfaction without disrupting production. So we propose that our disputes procedure should provide for pendulum arbitration to resolve disputes that cannot be settled by negotiation'. Although not finalised in exactly this form the eventual agreement leads to binding arbitration and in June 1986 the *Financial Times* and Sogat '82 resolved a pay and conditions in-house failure to agree by going down just this route.

So-called 'no strike' deals are, and will remain, rare. An EEF study[10] of industrial relations at shop floor level found that 52 out of 53 companies surveyed had no such deal. The reasons given suggested that none of them were contemplating such a move. They felt that they had no need, that the unions could not deliver or that the price would be too high. Most importantly there was a dislike of having responsibility for resolution taken away from the parties directly concerned.

There is no doubt that the changing approaches to relationships with employers is causing concern in the trade union movement. The fact is that many managements now see the important relationship as being that which it has with its employees rather than the formal relationship the industrial relations professionals have with the trade union officials. (This is very different to the 60s and 70s when managements often called in the officials to bring sanity into the proceedings.) By giving the supervisor a greatly enhanced role and by appointing people who have the capability of managing all aspects of their responsibility the day to day involvement of the professionals is reduced. By going for the commitment philosophy the relationship between employee and company changes. This, perhaps more than reduced membership because of unemployment and structural change, is the most significant long-term issue facing trade unions. There is no doubt that a different role is emerging for trade unions though it is difficult to predict what the conclusion will be. Alternatively there is an argument that this is all short term, the circle will turn and in ten years time we will be back to the attitude of the 50s and 60s. However, it is not possible to turn the clock back – changes *have* taken place and the base has been altered.

Trade unions are recognising that a change is taking place. Growing concern at these new managerial attitudes was voiced by TUC General Secretary, Norman Willis, in the Tom Mann Memorial Lecture in Coventry in March 1986. Relating directly to the activities of Japanese and American companies, particularly IBM, he said 'The concept in management circles is now human resource management seeking to secure commitment and flexibility from employees in exchange for relatively high pay and job security. This is far too fashionable'. Norman Willis sees this move as developing employee loyalty to the company rather than the union and makes the union job more difficult. 'The price of recognition – a single union, no strike compulsory arbitration agreement with Japanese firms, plus a legally enforceable agreement – may be too high a price to pay'.

It is this concept of loyalty to the company that so rankles left wing opponents of these new initiatives. Failing to realise that the intention is that all shall benefit, they attack what they believe are companies' attempts to usurp the traditional loyalties of worker to union. Writing in *Capital and Class*, the Journal of the Conference of Socialist Economists, Phillip Garrahan inaccurately described the Nissan procedures thus:

> While the agreement does not directly address a no strike option it effectively rules out industrial action by determining that ... if conciliation fails then disputes will go to final and binding arbitration. No official industrial action is provided for under the agreement during [the] three stages of negotiation, conciliation and arbitration. Indeed arbitration is deliberately ruled out so that unofficial action will be the only available recourse. It would be fair to say at the present moment that the company is making every effort to predict a loyal body of employees who would find unofficial action unthinkable.[11]

While the substance of this quotation is inaccurate the final sentence is clearly meant critically. To conceive of a workforce that has loyalty to the company and is therefore unlikely to strike is, to the left, highly undesirable. Mr Garrahan is though correct in his conclusion – companies *do* seek employee loyalty and they *do* want to develop an environment where industrial action is inconceivable! As in its attitude to quality control circles (see Chapter 5) the TGWU under the perceptive Ron Todd has put its finger on the precise pulse of the changing approach. Speaking at the Midlands Region conference of the Institute of Personnel Management in mid 1986 Mr Todd drew attention to the significant new fact of the 'powerful promotion by politicians and employers of ideas about how they want to see unions organised'. This resulted in a predetermination of negotiating rights by management policy in greenfield sites. Ron Todd described such practices as 'hollow vessels based on compulsion not consent' and attacking 'the long succession of Rambo heroes forging new industrial relations with the weapon of fear' he recognised that 'some very powerful forces in the economy and management circles seem to be redrawing the pitch as well as rewriting the traditional rules of the game'.

As in so many of these new initiatives only a few companies are affected. Dismissed by Ken Gill, TASS General Secretary as 'so marginal as to be almost irrelevant' (TASS Annual Conference April 1986) their significance lies not in the number of people covered by such Agreements but in the influence on thinking which they have. As IRRR has stated they are normally part of a total package which emphasises many different initiatives – and cannot be expected to succeed in the UK in isolation. It is this total change which the TASS General Secretary fears and in pouring scorn on the practice he, and other unions, are failing to face the challenge before them. While not exactly an idea whose time has come, so called 'no strike agreements' raise many questions for trade unions which they would prefer to go away.

One union which has seriously considered its future role is the GMB. While rejecting what it believes to be the EETPU gimmicks of no strike deals and pendulum arbitration the GMB nevertheless embraces many other aspects of the electricians approach. Its glossy promotional document 'Into 2000' offers single unionism (within TUC guidelines), single status, flexibility and binding arbitration (triggered by either party), 'our single union, single status agreement offers the opportunity of developing one of the best and most constructive forms of agreement available: an agreement based on realism and mutuality'. But the GMB goes further – it offers its professional services to new companies wishing to set up in the UK. Said General Secretary, John Edmonds, 'If a company ... wants to set up in this country they will know that not only will they get from us detailed knowledge of existing law, for instance, but also advice, help and support to set up a successful company within the British environment'. Through its white-collar section, MATSA, the GMB offers help and advice on health and safety matters, training at the union's colleges, pensions and other fringe benefits. And, while rejecting the concept of 'no strike deals', it does suggest agreements which provide for dispute resolution at the instigation of either side.

This view was echoed by Brenda Dean, General Secretary of SOGAT '82, when speaking at the 1986 Institute of Personnel Management Conference. Disclosing that her union was looking at the changing nature of the workforce, she predicted that in the

1990s more than 50 per cent of the workforce will be women with
many people working from home. She stated that unions will
have to be more responsive to their members' wishes. 'Our
people in the 1990s will have very different requirements. They
will not be interested in Brenda Dean negotiating their wages
because they will be self-employed but they may also feel isolated
so they will want our support.' This support, she believed, could
mean the provision of professional services and advice on issues
such as insurance, mortgages and pensions.

When combined with the EETPU marketing exercise of a
similar nature and the AEU's new approach on financial services
for members these new initiatives join a growing trend. (UCATT,
the construction workers' union, joined in November 1986 with
the launch of UCATT Financial Services.) But it does not answer
the question about the trade union role in the workplace in those
companies which have adopted the new approach.

Norman Willis expressed the problem at the 1986 IPM
conference. In what could come to be regarded as a watershed
speech he stated when speaking of the role of stewards, 'it does
mean that unions will have to give serious thought to re-
assessing their role – particularly what the implications are for
stewards of more emphasis by companies on communications,
on a sharper management style, on human resource development and on winning greater commitment from employees'.

This view of a possible change in the pattern of internal
relationships was echoed by ACAS in its 1986 Annual Report:

> There have been suggestions that personnel specialists are
> giving increasing weight to what is sometimes called 'human
> resource' management. By this is meant moves away from
> 'adversarial' views of work which stress the importance of
> management – union relationships, to an emphasis on
> developing organisational structures, training, pay and com-
> munication systems in ways which encourage individual
> employees to identify more fully with the aims and value of the
> business. How far such developments will prove practicable
> remains uncertain; if widely adopted they would raise further
> questions for trade unions about their future role and
> purpose.[12]

As in all such debates the conclusion will be somewhere
between the two extremes. Trade unionism will not disappear; it

will remain relevant but its role will change. How well it is able to recognise the need for and accommodate such change will significantly affect its continuing influence and role in our industrial society. The fact that this question is now at the top of the TUC agenda and is being vigorously debated augurs well for trade unionism. Even though many of the initial proposals from Norman Willis – particularly for a greater role for the TUC itself – are unacceptable to many trade unions it is the fact that the debate is taking place that is important. If, however, the debate is not concluded and the trade union movement drifts without a clear idea of the direction in which it is sailing, there can be little doubt that its relevance will be increasingly questioned by those people who really matter – the actual and potential membership.

10 Production Management– Enriching the Poor Relation

In the UK, manufacturing industry in general and production management in particular have long been regarded as the poor relation. The best graduates want to go into merchant banking, the professions, the Civil Service, the finance sector. If they think of industry or commerce it is the areas of marketing, sales, finance or personnel that attract – rarely production. The most common route for senior production personnel is to have worked their way up from the shop floor, having left school with few formal qualifications. While this is commendable to those who do progress, it does mean that the academic level of many is limited and thus their ability to progress to the most senior positions is restricted. While there will always be honourable exceptions, for the majority this is true.

This pattern was reflected in a 1985 study *Attracting the Brightest Students into Industry*.[1] The survey commented 'there was no significant understanding of the importance of business as the basis of wealth creation; no appreciation that it was a worthwhile career to follow, either in its own right or by its wealth creation process; or of the benefits it brings to the nation, the sick or the poor'. In the survey about 50 per cent of school children believed industry to be 'too routine and boring' and working in a factory was at the bottom of everyone's list of desirable jobs.

There can be little doubt that industry must shoulder much of the blame for the poor status it enjoys. Industry has failed to sell itself to the young. The traditional adversarial nature of British industrial relationships does not encourage the brightest young people to want to work in an environment in which they perceive it takes a battle to bring about the most innocuous of changes. The traditional nature of British education, with its emphasis on the arts rather than science, does little to demonstrate the fact that everything around us depends on manufacturing. Yet knowing of this attitude, industry does little to rectify it by actually going into schools. The Industrial Society's long-standing schools' liaison programme, The Challenge of Industry is one example of attempts to bridge the gap but is really no substitute for constant two-way exchanges between schools and industry, and visits to schools and universities by people actually working in industry. This means not only the managers but particularly young first line supervisors who are able to relate to the students and can demonstrate that it is possible to make progress rapidly and to have a meaningful and worthwhile career.

Challenge of Industry is of course not the only body in this field. Young Enterprise, Understanding British Industry, and the DTI's Industry Education Unit are but three more of a myriad of organisations totalling more than 80 which seek to bring together industry and education. But the very fact that there are so many, with one breath demonstrates the need and with the other helps only to confuse. To the embattled manager such bodies often have the appearance of well meaning social workers to be occasionally humoured but generally kept at arms length. When requests come for assistance it is usually the person who can best be spared who is assigned. If industry was really convinced of the need it would not require more than eighty organisations to help it!

Until the last few years companies themselves have constantly downgraded the role of production management. The growing number of functional departments have eroded the responsibilities of the first line supervisors. Personnel specialists have told them how to handle industrial relations matters, layout engineers have prepared the lay out of the job, cost accountants have determined the targets to be achieved and have berated the supervisors when they do not succeed, shop stewards have come between them and the workforce, claiming that it is their job, not the supervisors', to communicate with 'the members'. The list is endless and it is no wonder that a vicious circle has developed. Declining authority and responsibility make it less likely that capable people will wish to enter this area, and the fact that they are less capable means that the functional specialist will even more strongly 'advise'. Management pays lip service to the importance of the first line supervisors but often chooses to ignore them. It is no wonder that the foreman's job is often the one denigrated by all.

How does British industry go about changing the general perception? There is no lack of distinguished persons coming forward with their views – most of which are long on rhetoric and short on recipes. Sir John Harvey Jones, then Chairman of ICI, was more positive than most in his 1986 BBC Richard Dimbleby lecture (which was, incidentally, reprinted in full in the May 1986 *AEU Journal*). Widely praised at the time, Sir John emphasised a few often forgotten facts. Despite the tremendous run down of British industry we still export manufactured goods to the tune of £53 billion pounds – '25 per cent greater than the exports of banking, insurance and oil put together'. Manufacturing employs 5.5 million people and while its decline has been 60 per cent greater than the rest of the world the 'UK has been losing its share of the world market in services at nearly double the rate that it has in manufactures'. Quoting his own company, Sir John attacked the commonly held view that tourism might be our salvation 'In fact tourism's contribution to the balance of payment is only slightly positive. ICI's is positive to the tune of two thousand million pounds a year – so if we go under you will need to entertain at least another six million tourists a year' – a rather unfair comparison, but effective.

Most services depend very much on manufacturing for their infrastructure and there is no conceivable possibility of this country being able to survive without a strong manufacturing base. Sir John saw four elements to the future success of British manufacturing. 'First, exploiting our talent for science and invention with the emphasis on the word 'exploiting'. Second, putting to the best effect our ability to do international business. Third, getting a fair share of the brightest and best of our young into manufacturing and marketing – and enthusing them. And fourth, learning to be much more skilful at managing industrial change'.

While more practical than most such presentations, Sir John Harvey Jones did not really touch on the 'How' – he concentrated on the macro rather than the micro. Many who listened to or read his lecture would end up being inspired but not much wiser as to what they should do in their own company to bring about the much needed changes, so well defined. Put simply, the best people do not want to go into jobs where they believe they will have little real responsibility and even less status.

How then do we go about changing this status? There is no simple answer, but manufacturing industry cannot rely on other people. It has to look to itself to put its own house in order. And the vast majority of companies can only have influence within the confines of their own organisation. We have already seen in Chapter 6 that companies have to move from the view that they are in the employee relations business, the cost control business etc. to the point where they regard the indirect areas as providing a service to direct manufacturing. The task of the indirect areas is to make the task of production management easier – not to hamstring it with bureaucratic procedures which achieve consistency at the expense of initiative and which eventually become the masters – hampering flexibility and rapid response to changing circumstances.

It is imperative that there be a sea change in the role of the first line supervisor if British industry is to gain in status and become a sector which the brightest students regard as desirable. There are two main areas in which individual companies can influence this change. First of all the actual role of the supervisors must be considerably enhanced from its present lowly status and following from this their selection and training must be radically different.

There are signs that change is taking place. Some companies are actively seeking to redefine the role of the supervisor. One such company is Ford, which, recognising that the days of the foreman as a production chaser are numbered, established a Europe-wide study 'To build a vision of how employees throughout Manufacturing will need to be supported, guided and coached if the pressures for change and operational objectives are to be met'. In effect what will be the nature of leadership in the future. The fact that the words 'supported, guided and coached' are used gives a clear indication that Ford is considering a totally different role for the next generation of production supervision.

In another motor company, Jaguar, the role of the supervisor has been expanded. Jaguar's supervisor training programme includes elements on industrial engineering, presentation skills, finance and quality circles. Gone are the days (in some, but not all companies) when it was considered the shop steward's role to communicate with the *members*. More and more companies are beginning to realise, and then assert, that it is management's duty to communicate with *employees*. The development of team briefings and quality control circles means that often for the first time the first line supervisor is actually talking to his people and is leading discussions. But to do this you need the right people and then give them training. One of the reasons for lack of success in briefings is that the supervisor does not have the capability of handling such a situation. If he is schooled in the British tradition he has to learn how to move away from giving orders to consulting with people. And in such circumstances it is often perceived as a reduction in authority, whereas in reality it is giving the supervisor more, not less, responsibility and authority.

Kimberly Clark in its 16-year-old Tyneside site has made the conscious decision first to analyse and then to change the role of its first line supervisors. In moving from a traditional to a Group Leader role they decided that the new position would be responsible for output, costs, quality, safety, equipment management people and housekeeping; that they would build and encourage teamwork, make business decisions on shift and be responsible for communications. Among the qualities sought were the abilities to think analytically and communicate effectively; to have initiative, judgement, interpersonal sensitivity, flexibility, energy and, most importantly, to be able to make an impact. Kimberly Clark felt that it was possible to have all the positive attributes, to do all the right things, but still not have the personality that makes for effective leadership.

One company, Colemans of Norwich, reported by IDS,[2] greatly expanded the role of its supervisors encouraging them to play a greater role in identifying, defining and dealing with production problems and making them responsible for performance against the production plan. Colemans now includes among its supervisor candidates, people from areas other than production and others whose names are put forward by managers. Both Jaguar and Ford have attempted to recruit graduates into production supervision jobs but the numbers coming forward are limited, often because, as we have seen, the graduate perception of industry – and even more so of the role of production – is very low.

The problem in Britain is that few managements consider the supervisor position to be good experience and training for a move into 'real management'. They all too frequently base the selection decision on technical competency, ignoring the fact that rarely does such competency give a good indication of managerial capability and certainly is not a good predictor of the individual's capability to move into even higher positions.

The critical point is that for most companies and employees promotion to a foreman position is frequently regarded as the culmination of a 'career'. It *should* be regarded as virtually the beginning, and with the developing importance that is being placed on the role of the supervisor, it is no longer sufficient to regard the shop floor as being the sole source of recruitment.

While it is always possible to identify exceptions, the general trend in British industry has been that the 'best' shop floor workers have been those who have been promoted to foreman. The most important factor has been the technical ability of the individual and often little thought has been given to his ability to actually manage the job and even less training has been given so as to equip him. Consequently the great majority of people who move off the shop floor are ill-prepared to handle the next stage, let alone progress up the management hierarchy. Because of this, and to a certain extent it is a chicken and egg situation, managerial trust of its first line foreman is very low, the levels of responsibility given to the position are minimal and consequently the high-potential people do not want to take such positions.

How then do we turn the vicious circle into one of virtue? There are three elements to the answer – status and responsibility, authority and salary. All are interrelated and none can be considered in isolation from the other elements discussed throughout this book. It is easiest to begin with money.

In 1984 the average salary of first line supervisors was around £7.900. In British industry the differential between the manual worker and his supervisor is often narrow, and it is not unknown for the supervised to take home more money than the supervisor – particularly when piece rates, overtime and shift payments are included. Frequently in cash terms there is little incentive for a shop floor worker to seek promotion to what is often a glorified progress chaser with little real authority.

We have seen that in Nissan we regard the production team as being central to the success of the enterprise and have already inferred much of the role and responsibilities of the people responsible for those teams. Thus we decided from the very beginning that the production supervisor would be at exactly the same level in the organisation as the professional engineers and administrators and, among other things, this means that salary levels are the same. What you pay someone is the most overt indication of the value you place on that person. To say, therefore, that the company places great importance on the calibre of its supervision and then pays them less than other people would be a clear example of actions not living up to words. Thus we established one level encompassing supervisors, engineers and controllers and placed all on exactly the same salary range. As, essentially, this range was determined by the rate necessary to attract experienced motor industry engineers, it results in supervisors being paid within a range of £13,250 to £16,530 (from 1 January 1987). This is higher than the motor industry rate and considerably in excess of the North-eastern rate but is entirely justified when considering the role and responsibilities of Nissan supervisors.

In order to enhance the responsibility and role of production supervision it is essential to give back many of the responsibilities that have been taken away over the years. Nissan supervisors are responsible for making the decisions on who will work for them; they have full responsibility for quality, housekeeping and much maintenance. Within obvious constraints they lay out their work area and material arrives lineside where *they* want it to come. They have the responsibility and authority continuously to improve work methods and timing – and to resolve problems. They develop their own process sheets and control their own costs. It is the supervisor who communicates with the group. Above all they are the genuine leaders of the group, motivating people not through mechanistic control systems imposed by Finance or Personnel 'because the foreman is no good and cannot be trusted' but through their ability as managers. One simple example of this latter point (discussed more fully in Chapter 7): it is not uncommon in British industry for manual workers, who clock in late, to be stopped pay on a minute by minute basis. The attitude develops 'If I'm five minutes late I lose five minutes pay and the company loses five minutes work – that's a fair trade'. Then the Personnel Department comes along and establishes a vastly complex lateness disciplinary procedure which talks about 'four times late in a month – first written warning, four times late in second month – second written warning', etc. Employees soon get to know how to work the system. The poor supervisor has little say except to hand out the letters which are often automatically generated.

However real lateness control is nothing to do with mechanistic systems – it is all about giving the supervisor responsibility for motivating his people. Neither Continental nor Nissan automatically stops pay for lateness but we give to supervisors the authority to do so if they believe their people are taking advantage of the system. There is no better method of controlling lateness than the supervisor knowing his people and that, say, Thursday night is the darts team night. A quiet word to the potential recalcitrant can do far more than a lifetime of clocking on and stopping pay.

If the money is right and the responsibilities and authority are as described, the status part falls into place easily – provided the people doing the job are of the calibre necessary to properly fulfill the responsibilities. Many companies are now paying increased attention to the method of selection of production (and other) management. With the changing role, 'buggin's turn' is no longer enough; technical ability, by itself, is insufficient.

The IDS Study *Supervisors of Manual Workers*[3] reported on companies which have become more sophisticated in their selection of supervisors. Coleman's of Norwich has changed from a process which used the shop floor as its sole source to one which includes other groups such as quality controllers or engineers. Jaguar cars has introduced a selection procedure for shop floor workers which includes a battery of aptitude tests, panel interviews and performance review. From 1979 Ford changed its supervisor selection process and introduced one day assessment centres whereby candidates who had successfully completed a battery of psychometric tests took part in a number of exercises dealing with realistic production situations including exercises on scheduling, counselling employees with bad work habits, resolution of quality problems and so on. Explained Paul Roots, then Ford's Director of Employee Relations, in *Works Management*,[4] selecting good supervisors is the most positive way of maintaining labour relations. 'It's the one thing that has an effect in any industry'.

In any organisation it is an essential, though often omitted, task to define requirements before recruiting. It remains the easiest thing to determine such requirements in terms of technical ability. Indeed we could have filled up Nissan with supervisors from the British motor manufacturing industry, who were technically competent, but on careful analysis were found to be lacking in the managerial and personal qualities necessary to work in the environment we were seeking to create.

The process had to start however before recruiting the supervisors. It was essential in a company start-up situation that the people who were to build the plant to build the cars, knew something about building cars. We simply had no time to be able to teach the managers the technical fundamentals of the job they would be doing. Nevertheless we emphasised the difference of approach. The text of the advertisement for production managers included such phrases as

> A cornerstone of our management philosophy is that individual employees are the key to quality and productivity. Required qualities include enthusiasm and commitment to success – positive attitude towards new technology and systems and sufficient mental and physical vitalty and stamina to introduce them successfully – sense of quality consciousness.

While succumbing a little to the advertising agent's enthusiasm, the text at least indicated the beginnings of a philosophy which at that time had not fully emerged.

Typically in the British motor manufacturing industry, the individual who is able to work his way from the shop floor to being a production manager is not often imbued with the qualities Nissan was seeking. Thus, many technically competent people fell at this hurdle. We were in fact looking for experienced managers who saw that there was a different way of running a car plant – people who wanted the opportunity of putting into practice 'all those ideas' that they would like to introduce if they ever had the chance!

The method of selecting managers was nothing revolutionary. With the help of MSL we were able to appoint a group of high calibre, highly motivated managers. The real difference came when we started our supervisor recruitment. By this time – Spring 1984 – we had firmed up the philosophy of how the company should be run and wished to select people who had a basic empathy with that philosophy. However good, technically, they might be, if they did not have a commitment to 'Doing things a better way' we were not interested. Provided people had a good general engineering or production base that could be adapted and developed to motor manufacturing techniques, the personal qualities were more important than specialist knowledge. Thus technical expertise was necessary but not sufficient.

The advertisement for supervisors was headlined:

Supervision with Nissan *will* be different

Emphasising the tripod of teamworking, flexibility and quality consciousness we stated that we were looking for people who had these qualities themselves and the capability of developing such qualities in others. We received 3500 applications for 22 jobs! With the help of MSC Jobs Centre staff we were able to reduce these to 200, all of whom were interviewed. As a result of this process 75 survived. It was then that the interesting part started.

All people with a responsibility for selecting others believe they are good interviewers. 'I can tell within five minutes if someone is any good or not'. While this might be true at the extremes it is not easy to choose, from a large number of good candidates, those who have the personal qualities you are seeking. Despite their belief in the infallibility of their personal judgement, most interviewers can (if honest to themselves) point to a number of dreadful mistakes they have made. It is salutory to remind ourselves that every time we criticise someone's work performance, that person has usually been selected through the interview process. Thus we criticise not only the individual but also the selection process and the person who made the selection decision.

Because of the importance of the supervisor position, and the number being recruited at the same time, Nissan decided that it should do everything possible to minimise the chances of making mistakes. We therefore developed our own assessment centre, a technique whereby a number of candidates undertake a variety of tasks so that their performance can be judged by various people from different angles. There is no doubt that the assessment centre process is both time-consuming and expensive and at the beginning was viewed with some scepticism. However at the end of the process, when we had spent something over 100 manager days selecting 22 supervisors, the effect on the participating managers was like a conversion on the road to Damascus. To them, now, there is no other effective method.

A key role in the Nissan supervisors assessment centre was played by occupational psychologists, Saville and Holdsworth. The company has both contributed to and benefited from the growth of interest in the more sophisticated methods of assessment and selection. Psychological testing is of course nothing new. According to Peter Saville, tests of ability and temperament can be traced back to the Old Testament 'where Gideon, faced with too many volunteers for his army, reduced the numbers by telling them how dangerous war can be and then instructing the remaining group to drink at the nearest stream; those who knelt down to lap the water failed, but those who kept alert by cupping the water as they drank, he selected'.[5]

Nissan, in its test programme for supervisors, did not attempt to distinguish the old concept of basic intelligence from that of acquired knowledge. The nature-nurture debate has long been concluded in favour of those who accept that both inherited characteristics and environmental factors play a part in forming the whole person. Equally there is no such thing as a totally culture-free test. In any case we were not seeking to distinguish basic intelligence in a culture-free environment. Our supervisors would be very much part of the culture. We did however attempt to distinguish the results of formal education and training (attainment tests) and the ability to acquire further knowledge or skills (aptitude tests). Measures of aptitude do, of course, depend to a great extent on prior knowledge of the numerical or verbal systems on which they are based, but they do, however, try to avoid specialist knowledge which very few candidates would have had the opportunity to acquire.

In attempting to measure attainment we used a number of tests from the Saville and Holdsworth Technical Test Battery – verbal reasoning, numerical reasoning and mechanical comprehension. We were seeking to measure their verbal ability, reasoning skills with numbers and the understanding of basic mechanical principles and the ability to handle concepts and problem resolution. These tests have been used by other motor manufacturers in assessing applicants for supervisory positions, and therefore a norm score for such applicants has been established. In this area of knowledge and ability we were therefore able to directly relate our candidates against the industry norm. Needless to say the selected Nissan supervisors far exceeded this norm!

The fourth element of the assessment centre was the Occupational Personality Questionnaire – a personality assessment technique specifically related to work performance. Then a group exercise during which observed groups of six had to work together to produce a factory layout, using a certain amount of data (interestingly, after the event the successful supervisors stated that they felt that this part of the process told more about them than any other single aspect and asked to use it in selecting the team leaders who would be working for them). We held a formal buffet dinner at which specified topics were introduced for discussion, we mixed informally with the candidates and at the end of the day brought together all individual reports on each of the candidates. These were processed and a 1 to 5 rating given on each section. Each rating was then entered on to a wall chart together with any specific comments.

The interviews that followed the next day were intended to explore in greater depth areas of concern that had been raised during the assessments or, if there were contradictions, to explore the differences and attempt to determine the correct version. The applicants were given the opportunities of commenting on what had been said about them and often, when shown the assessments, it was revealing to see how they coped with the information. Very few thought the assessments inaccurate – indeed the overall response was one of amazement that so much had been discovered. Finally, all candidates were medically examined by an occupational physician, a process which resulted in a surprisingly high failure rate.

The essential point in this process is that you are trying to identify trends. No single aspect of the assessment is by itself wholly reliable – any more than the standard interview – but taken together, patterns do begin to emerge. With no cross reference during the process, we found it fascinating how specific points relating to individuals would keep occurring frequently in a different form but sometimes in almost identical terms. It would be nice, of course, if one could then pick out a particular part of the procedure, which would be one hundred per cent valid and then use only that. Unfortunately by attempting that, we would quickly return to the interview syndrome, although this time it might be the group exercise!

Thus no one, least of all the psychologists, regards these assessments as being infallible. They are of value in so far as they add to the body of knowledge. But two interesting postscripts – we had a number of comments after the event from unsuccessful candidates that they felt they had been given every opportunity to present themselves in a fair way and that this reflected well on the Company. Second, in the Sir Michael Edwardes era at British Leyland, considerable use was made of psychological testing on BL managers (Sir Michael's previous company, Chloride, was an early user of such tests), in an attempt to determine what redeployments were necessary. However, as a result of the assessment process, many managers left the company and the tests were perceived by many as being 'pass' or 'fail' and were resented. It could be that too much reliance was placed on one aspect of what should be a multi-faceted process.

With the process complete there began the task of selecting 22 from the 75. The assessment centre had allowed most managers to see most candidates and with assistance from the Saville and Holdsworth team we started to eliminate the obvious rejects and select those who everyone agreed were obvious choices. It was interesting to compare the peformance of the motor industry candidates, who for the most part exhibited the traits and personality that makes for success in that environment, but were not necessarily the characteristics Nissan was seeking. Frequently the candidates previously known to our managers, and commended by them for their technical ability, fell by the wayside and it is a tribute to the commitment of our managers that they readily recognised this. On the other hand the strength of many of the local candidates was impressive.

When examining the successful candidates, a number of interesting points emerged. They were young – the youngest was 23 and the oldest 38. They are highly qualified – several to degree or equivalent levels. None were unemployed and only six of the 22 were from the British motor manufacturing industry. This profile gave a few surprises to our Japanese colleagues, who were used to foremen being appointed after 18 years on the production line. However, by their dedication, enthusiasm, ability and willingness to learn they impressed everyone. Particularly their performance in Japan, during several months of vigorous training, demonstrated that it does not always need many years on a line before you can be put in charge of it.

Another North-eastern company, Kimberley Clark, went even further than Nissan when selecting people for its newly established position of Group Leader. Having defined the new role, the company developed a multi-faceted process which it applied to both internal and, subsequently, external candidates. Stage one involved interviews, aptitude tests and, for the internal candidates, internal references. Stage two was a two day residential assessment, the first day comprising of questionnaires, two minute talks, case studies, information exchange, team work projects and what they call 'fun events'. The second day was made up of outdoor tests of the '5 gallon drum across a ravine' and 'building a raft to cross a lake' variety. Interestingly they found that the outdoor exercises gave them considerable additional information rather than simply duplicating the results of the first day's tests.

Without doubt, however, the single biggest task for Nissan was to select its manufacturing staff. Being very much aware of the likely enormous response, we gave considerable thought to the logistics of the exercise and in particular we needed to develop some method of quickly and accurately sorting people into those who could go through for more detailed consideration and those who could be rejected on the basis of their application form.

Such was the success of the assessment centre, that we developed variations of it for selecting the Team Leaders and subsequently, without the OPQ, the manufacturing staff. While more practically based, these procedures were no less demanding and depended very much on our newly appointed supervisors working with the local Wearside College in designing and administering the aptitude and practical test programmes. We received about 1000 applications for the 40 Team Leader positions and 11,500 for 300 manufacturing staff posts. The selection process attracted national media attention. Under the heading 'Nissan calls many but chooses few', Peter Hetherington in *The Guardian* referred to the approach as being 'the most sophisticated ever adopted by a Company in Britain... The six-stage process takes about seven hours and few candidates will quibble with the cautionary note on Nissan recruitment advertisements "Very few people will reach our standards". – It is more like a pre-entry programme for budding Army Officers'.[6]

This process had in fact started much earlier, for we prepared a fact sheet to go out with the manufacturing staff application forms. Included in this fact sheet were both the attractions of working for Nissan and the hard facts about work on a production line. Not only did we say 'we believe that attention to quality, pride in the job and spirit of teamwork and cooperation within Nissan will be second to none. For those with the right attitude and motivation it will be a satisfying and rewarding environment. We look for and expect individual contribution to continually improve the company and its productivity and quality' but also 'We do not intend to mislead people about the role of Manufacturing Staff or the environment in which they will work. All applicants should carefully consider the following points:

- The pace of work will be dictated by a moving production line and will be very demanding.

- Work assignments will be carefuly defined and will be repetitive.

- Protective clothing will be necessary for some jobs.

- You may be moved onto a new operation or transferred into a different Department at very short notice.'

This we felt would put off a number of applicants, who were attracted by the name Nissan. The aura which had built up around us in the North-east and the headline of our advertisement, which continued the theme 'Working with Nissan will be different.' (We had incidentally deliberately used the word 'with' Nissan as opposed to 'for' Nissan, which, while probably unnoticed by many, did indicate what we were about and emphasised the care with which we developed our total strategy).

Not only did we prepare the fact sheet to go out with the standard application form, but we also developed a separate questionnaire which had to be completed by all applicants. Our discussions, particularly with other companies, had convinced us that we needed systems which not only dissuaded the basically uninterested from applying but also allowed an objective, effective and rapid first sort through the applications. Bearing in mind that the standard Nissan application form is four sides and that our internal resources were limited – particularly as many of our supervisors were in Japan during this initial stage – we developed a complementary one-sided tick box sheet, which asked about twenty questions. Each question had several answers eg.

How many miles do you live from the Nissan plant?	Under 5 ☐	5–15 ☐	15–25 ☐	25+ ☐

A final sheet of paper given to all candidates was a computer record card, which had again to be completed, giving basic information to be fed into our computer control system, which we had decided was essential to ensure that we could monitor and control the whole selection process.

Thus Nissan candidates received four separate pieces of paper totalling seven sides – enough to put off many of the less committed. And it did just that. We had agreed with the MSC that distribution of application forms would be through the Job Centres alone. On the day of the advertisement all North-east Job Centres were flooded with potential applicants, for although we advertised only in the local newspapers, the fact that we were now advertising for manual workers received saturation news coverage. Co-ordinated by Harry Townsend, the Washington Job Centre Manager, who had done an excellent job for us with supervisor and team leader recruitment, even the local Job Centre staff were surprised by the initial response. In all some 20 000 application forms and associated material were given out, mainly within a few days of the advertisement appearing. But our attempts at dissuading the less enthusiastic worked. The actual number returned was 11 500, a 57.5 per cent return rate.

For two weeks following the advertisement we worked with MSC Staff in sorting the applications. With the aim of reducing the 11 000 to around 2000, we used the single sheet questionnaire to determine the number of 'undesirable' responses and were able to sort applicants into piles according to the results. Although a mechanical process, it did have the effect of very quickly allowing us to undertake the initial determination. However every single applicant was subsequently individually reviewed on the basis of the full application form. Experience tells us that selecting on the basis of written forms is not infallible, so to do so on the basis of a tick box questionnaire is not only unfair on the candidates but also at the same time could lose many potentially suitable applicants. We therefore insisted that every application form was not only marked but was also reviewed by at least two Nissan supervisors and/or managers.

It was as a result of this process that we reduced the numbers to 1900, who then were started on the next stages of the selection process. In this we were very much influenced by the experience of our sister company in the United States. Although we had neither the time nor resources of our colleagues in Tennessee, visits by both the author and the Director of Production convinced us that in order to be successful in our recruitment we had to apply a high degree of practical testing prior to actual hire.

We determined, however, that we would implement a process which would aim to predict the same factors as the US demonstrated. We could not, however, interview 1900 remaining candidates. Therefore we devised a programme whereby all 1900 would be given aptitude tests (Industrial Psychology Inc's Numerical and Fluency Tests and Bennett Mechanical Comprehension) during a series of sessions lasting throughout October and November 1985 followed, importantly, by a tea and biscuits session, which enabled our supervisors and managers to talk informally with the candidates. As a result of this process we aimed to reduce the numbers by about 50 per cent.

In fact, over 1100 went through to the next stage, which was a practical skill module, which had been devised by our supervisors and was aimed at testing the skill level of candidates, their aptitude, their ability to follow instructions and most important of all their learning capacity. Based on a constructed rig the tests involved reading instructions and then using hands, power tools and ordinary tools to complete a series of practical exercises in a variety of physical positions, including stooping and overhead work, bending and stretching and manual dexterity. At all times we were also looking for their attitude and approach to problems and this was further reinforced by a general discussion involving the candidates and supervisors.

Such sophisticated selection methods are becoming more commonplace. As part of its changing style brought about after the involvement of PA Management Consultants, Austin Rover has developed a two day assessment centre to take place over weekends. ARG is not simply looking for manual skills, but also whether potential employees identify with the aims and philosophy of the Company. Because of the numbers involved it was not possible to go to such lengths when selecting people for the new Rover 800 line but, said Andy Barr, ARG's Managing Director (Operations), 1200 workers had been selected after 'a total assessment including interviews, team involvement exercises and practical exercises'.

Inmos determined from the start that it would have a highly selective recruitment procedure with the most important criteria being the candidates' motivation. This is particularly important where a high level of individual responsibility is necessary to ensure proper quality levels and therefore production workers undertook a number of general ability and manual dexterity tests in addition to the interview before being chosen.

The Whitbread Magor Brewery interviewed selected applicants twice, took up two written references and gave a full medical examination. The second interview was conducted by two managers and included an assessment of whether or not the candidate would fit into the team, and a visit to the work area. When the brewery initially opened, they were able to select 250 staff from some 3000 applicants.

Carreras Rothman at Spennymoor received more than 12,000 applications and based a manager at the local Job Centre for several months to conduct preliminary interviews. Second interviews were carried out at the factory and one out of nine was selected on the basis of tested manual dexterity, adaptability and the ability to work as a member of a team. It is not insignificant that two thirds of the chosen workforce were aged 34 or below with few over 50 being successful. Carreras Rothman found that younger people did better on the adaptability and openness criteria.

Fisher Body, based near Belfast, adopted the General Motors QWL philosophy and consequently paid great attention to selecting people who they believed would fit in with such an approach. Following an initial interview, and a series of NIIP tests, short listed candidates were invited to an assessment centre session, lasting around four hours, designed to 'measure several factors in order to determine, as much as possible, how well the individual skills match the stated goals and philosophy'. The factors on which individuals were rated included interpersonal skills, trust, participation and involvement, individual's organisational needs, planning and organising, analytical ability, oral communication skill, decision making and persuasiveness/influence. Very interestingly they included fitters and assembly workers among the assessors.

In describing the experience of Whitbread, Carreras Rothman and Fisher Body, IDS summarised the characteristics that the employers were seeking:

- Reliability
- Flexibility
- Openness and good 'interpersonal skills.'[7]

Clearly new management styles need new-style people to be managed, but also there is a clear desire to start off differently and to develop from within rather than have to import the bad habits from previous sites or companies. If you are convinced that group working or team building is important for the success of the operation, you do not start off by recruiting the loners, who will not fit in, or the awkward squad, who will try to destroy.

Paul Hill's *Towards a New Philosophy of Management*[8] dwelt at length on the selection process, which was devised in conjunction with the supervisors. With 3000 applicants for 156 jobs, Shell UK included the following words in the letter inviting candidates to complete an application form: 'We are now recruiting operating staff, who will be trained on site for approximately six months. No-one should underestimate the difficulties that are bound to arise in starting up a refinery of this complexity. We are seeking men, who will accept the challenge of these difficulties and who will prove adaptable to changing circumstances. We shall depend a great deal upon the individual effort and sense of responsibility of each member of the staff, who will – after training – be required to work without close supervision'. The recruitment programme that followed directly involved the supervisors and, according to Paul Hill, 'An important element in this process was to obtain from the applicants, at their first interview, their reaction to the sort of responsible flexible jobs which were envisaged for operators, so that people to whom this did not appeal could withdraw from the follow-up interview'. Once the teams were assembled, it was the supervisors who trained their teams. It is a pity that the Shell Teesport refinery has closed – a clear indication that the market is stronger than management.

IBM has always taken great care in selecting its managers – which in that company is the name given to all employees who have supervisory responsibilities for others. Among their criteria for selection, IBM includes, in addition to technical ability and performance, the ability to motivate employees and adopt a consultative management style. Reported in *Industrial Relations Review and Report*, Optical Fibres established a rigorous selection procedure, with all short listed candidates being given two or three lengthy interviews, and thus being seen by up to six people. 'For technical jobs one interview would concentrate on job knowledge, whilst in another interview the applicant's attitudes and personality would be assessed in relation to his or her ability to work as a team member. The most important personal quality sought by the panel was a flexibility of approach enabling the individual to adapt to flexible working practices and the need for updating of skills and knowledge to keep pace with technological change. As a result, Optical Fibres established a workforce which it would describe as consisting of positive and progressive minded individuals'. Also important to Optical Fibres was the requirement to select a workforce with a high standard of education, and as a result the majority of process workers are 'O' level or good-CSE qualified. In the maintenance department, employees are qualified to technical engineer standard.

This considerable emphasis on the selection method for production personnel is a clear indication of the importance of the job. It not only achieves the object of selecting high quality people, but also demonstrates to the world at large that production is not something that is the last refuge – the place to go to if no other alternative is available. By emphasising its importance, we intend to make our contribution to breaking the vicious circle, and turn production management from a low status, low responsibility, low quality, low pay profession to one with high status, responsibility, quality and pay. Production management must become a profession which high-calibre graduates choose in preference to the alternatives currently at the top of their list. We expect to recruit engineering graduates who can move in and out of engineering, design and production management. Indeed, we would wish to go further and have complete interchange, as far as is practical, between engineering, production and administration. One pleasing aspect was that the first promotion in Nissan was of a Senior Engineer to a Production Manager; the Senior Engineer was replaced by a Supervisor, the Supervisor by a Technician and the Technician by a Manufacturing Staff member. That is a pretty good beginning!

Conclusion: Human Resources – A Strategy

There is a great danger in trying to pull together the many complex threads that have been discussed throughout this book. The greatest of all is that the neat summary can suggest that there is an all-embracing formula which will apply under all conditions, at all times and in all organisations. This is simply not true and, hopefully, this has been made clear in the preceding chapters. Equally dangerous is to suggest that elements can be extracted from the whole and be successfully introduced without consideration of their interdependence with other factors.

However, with these provisos it may be helpful to attempt to pull things together, for it is essential that we look at the 'people' part of our businesses in the same way as we look at investment or product – and that is *strategically*. The essential questions are 'Where are we now?', 'Where do we want to be in, say, five years time?' and 'How do we get from "here" to "there"?' Unless we actually think strategically about what the Americans call 'human resources' we will continue with crisis management, from negotiation to negotiation, and will end up with all the costs of change and few of the benefits. It is no use saying 'It's alright for you – you had a greenfield site' or 'You had a major injection of American capital' or 'You had to change or die'. The special circumstances of some are not an excuse for doing nothing. The most difficult organisation in which to introduce change is the one which is doing reasonably well and sees no immediate reason to change. A gardener once said 'If you weed before you need to weed you will never *need* to weed'. In business, if you change before change is thrust upon you, you will never *need* to change!

All any company can do is what is right for it in its circumstances. But there are enough examples of established companies in the UK that are not foreign owned, nor in electronics nor on greenfield sites to suggest that change can be successfully introduced in a variety of industries. Eldridge Pope & Co, the family-owned Dorchester-based brewery, stated in its 1985 Directors Report, 'We invest large amounts of time and money in involving employees in the operation and success of the business, and our objective is quite simply increasing success as measured by growing profits. It is profits which sustain the present and equip the future giving prosperity and security to the whole team, shareholders and employees alike. A happy and satisfying working life is a by-product which is of course closely linked'. In a totally different business, Hardy Spicer, manufacturers of components for the motor industry, decided to develop their own 'greenfield' *within* a long established manufacturing plant. By literally building a fence to divide the new from the old and then by specially selecting the people to work in the new area on new equipment with new training and new requirements they have successfully demonstrated that it is possible to change – but they have done so in *their* way.

In the United States Pratt & Whitney has examined its 60-year-old culture. The company concluded that it was product-orientated, achieved quality through inspection, saw its people as an expendable resource, believed in management by control and used one-way communication. Now the value system has changed to one where the customer is the centre of the universe, quality is built in and people are regarded as the single most important part of the organisation and its only appreciable asset. The purpose of management is to facilitate and thus recognise that the largest single repository of ideas is the workforce, so 'two-way communication' is of paramount importance.[1]

But in all such instances, Eldridge Pope, Hardy Spicer, Nissan, Continental, Pratt & Whitney and the many other quoted companies, common principles do emerge. Very rarely is there anything revolutionary. Indeed in the individual components there is little that is new – there is no point in reinventing the wheel – and often it can best be described as getting the basics right. But what *are* the basics? The beginning must be to establish an objective which states something like

> Our objective is to establish an atmosphere of mutual trust, cooperation and commitment in which all employees can identify with the aims and objectives of the company and which encourages and recognises the individual contribution of all.

It is, of course, easy to write down but very difficult to achieve. Also, it implies that the company knows what its aims and objectives are – not something that is always explicit!

Now comes the difficult part. Because I have argued for the holistic approach in which all elements are interdependent, where does one break into the circle? Central to the Nissan approach has been the concept of giving back to line management and supervisors many of the responsibilities that have been taken away from them over the years by the bright young people in the indirect departments. Chapter 10, 'Enriching the poor relation', discussed the reasons for this and the problems to which it has led – not least being that the best people, if they want to enter industry at all, rarely wish to work in production.

Industry cannot blame anyone else for its poor status. If it is to attract high quality people at all levels it must create meaningful jobs at all levels which combine high authority, responsibility and salaries. Specifically in production areas (but also elsewhere) Nissan has given to supervisors the responsibility for

- selecting the people who will work for them and then being the first person to advise the successful candidate – this is the start of the bond and the first element in the team building process.

- communicating all matters on a face to face basis to the team – this is done primarily at the five minute meeting at the start of shift. Most of the information originates from the supervisor and is conveyed in *his* way, not a centralised 100 per cent accurate way. If it is worth telling it must be told quickly. The Company newspaper can only handle the less important, less immediate matters.

- total responsibility for quality. The supervisor and his team build in quality. There are no 'In process inspectors' whose job it is to minutely check other peoples work. The production team checks its own work and passes it to its 'customer' – the next person in the process.

- ensuring continuous improvement (*kaizen*) both of quality and productivity. The management task is to encourage proposals for improvement from people in the team, to assess them and then, wherever possible, have the team (not an outside group) introduce the change. This can mean the team itself writing or amending process sheets or fabricating new equipment or facilities. Once the team's enthusiasm is tapped there is no end to the improvements they can come up with. They are the people who know the job better than anyone else.

- maintenance. If the team can troubleshoot or fix a problem they do so. If they cannot they will work with the maintenance people when they come along.

- achieving high levels of attendance and timekeeping. No-one clocks and no-one is stopped pay for lateness or absenteeism but to be late or absent is rare. Attendance is little to do with sickness and a lot to do with motivation.

- training on the job. It is the supervisor's task to ensure that he has a matrix of skills so that every job can be done by every team member to varying levels; eg within quality standard; quality plus standard time; quality, standard time and train others; quality, standard time, train others and troubleshoot.

- balancing the job, responsibility for costs and understanding the myriad of other technical responsibilities that are given to him.

The essential point is that the supervisor has to change from being a progress chaser to being a leader of a team and he cannot do that unless first he is a member of the team. Thus as discussed on page 87 all supervisors have meeting areas which combine a meeting point with rest area, tea room, social area, work place (for administrative tasks and discussions), communication centre and so on. In this area the supervisor has his desk, holds his morning meeting and enjoys his tea break. Theoretically the supervisor is also responsible for discipline and resolving grievances but if he gets everything else right he does not have formal discipline cases or grievances raised – he has the authority and ability to sort out any potential problems on an informal basis.

Contained within this description of the supervisor's responsibility are most of the elements of the Nissan tripod – teamworking and commitment, quality and flexibility. Teamworking is not group working nor interdependence – it is about everyone working in the same direction. Flexibility is not about moving people around rapidly – it is expanding everyone's responsibilities as much as possible. Quality is not about inspection or suggestions schemes or quality control circles – it is about developing an absolute commitment at every level in the organisation that quality is the prime objective.

While the supervisor's role has so far been emphasised, this is perhaps because it is the job that has been most neglected by British industry. But the supervisor will only motivate his people in the way proposed if he himself is motivated by his manager and the manager in turn by his director. The chain is as strong as its weakest link. But to develop this philosophy the managers and supervisors must be fully involved. Only by involving people in determining that you wish to involve people will you get real commitment. Top management decreeing that 'We will involve people' is self contradictory and will not work. And above all – do not keep talking about it – just do it!

So often we seek to negotiate Employee Involvement or establish complex training programmes or send people on team building courses. To go down these routes invites antagonism from trade unions who see it as a device to bypass their 'right' to be the only people who talk to 'their members'. To send people on courses makes something special of what should be a normal part of the job. Involving people can begin by simply asking someone to sort out a problem or find a better way of doing the job. It can mean the receptionist knowing the quality level being achieved or it can mean a group of managers examining future organisational changes as the company evolves. The message must be 'Involve people in those areas in which they can directly contribute and keep them informed about those areas in which they cannot'.

So often in British industry we erect our own barriers to prevent progress. The traditional differences between 'staff' and 'hourly paid' divides employees into first and second class citizens. Put simply, you do not get a first-class response from second-class citizens – why should somebody who is treated as though he cannot be trusted, who is regarded as being 'economic man' motivated only by money, act any differently. The Nissan way is to treat everyone as first-class citizens – to get the basic pay and conditions right and achieve involvement and commitment by the way people are managed. But common terms and conditions does not only mean the same pension scheme or a single dining room. It also means a single integrated salary structure in which manual workers, supervisors, engineers, administrators are placed together. It means that if you have salary ranges and progression on merit for white-collar workers you also have it for manual workers – and that then means developing an objective method of assessing performance that is capable of application to all groups of employees. Very importantly it also means a single integrated bargaining body on which representatives of *all* employees sit together. Nissan calls this the Company Council and the elected representatives hopefully consider that what unites them because they are all employees of the same company is stronger than what might divide them because one represents manufacturing staff, another supervisors, another administrators, etc.

Another traditional barrier is the job evaluation scheme which causes companies to spend vast amounts of the time erecting a monolith comprising job specifications, review bodies, appeals committees etc. The end result is a system which provides precise details of the responsibilities of each job but serves to restrict (rather than expand) what people do. In the end we have scores (or hundreds) of job titles, numerous grading levels, many steps from top to bottom and the preservation of the system becomes more important than responding rapidly to changing technology, processes or market conditions. While we cannot (and should not) change existing systems overnight, companies should ask themselves the question 'Is the tail wagging the dog?' In Nissan we have *no* job descriptions, do not employ a myriad of different types of, for example, engineers. We employ only 'Engineers' and 'Senior Engineers' and at any time the Senior may be undertaking work that is less complex, more complex or of the same complexity as the Engineer. But the Senior Engineer is in charge. Engineers, Supervisors and Controllers are at the same level in the organisation so that the structure does not mitigate against mobility. There are only two manual worker job titles – Technician and Manufacturing Staff – every job in a car manufacturing plant can be contained within these titles.

It is within this overall 'culture' that the formal relationship with the trade union exists. Nissan's single union deal with the AEU is designed to be supportive of the policy. It emphasises quality and recognises the value of the contribution each individual can make. It treats all staff as responsible adults but also provides that those who abuse this trust can be properly and fairly dealt with. Although within the Agreement there is a grievance procedure, by July 1987, not one grievance had been registered. By giving real responsibility to supervisors, by appointing people who are genuine members of the team as well as leaders of it, grievances are minimised and those which do occur can be properly resolved where they should be – between the people directly affected. As soon as the grievance is resolved higher up the line, the supervisor's authority is diminished.

We have seen in Chapter 9 that there is no such thing as a 'no strike' agreement. Under the Nissan–AEU deal there is in fact a point at which industrial action would be constitutional. However, the Agreement does provide for automatic reference to ACAS for conciliation following an in house failure to agree and then, by joint agreement, reference to binding arbitration on a pendulum basis. But the key point is that both the company and the union are totally committed to resolving problems in-house – and as early as possible. When there is a recognition that the success of the company and the people it employs are mutually interdependent there must come a recognition that what unites is stronger than what divides. There then comes a genuine commitment to resolve problems rather than score points. At July 1987 there had been no in-house failures to agree.

A further essential element making for success – indeed a necessary condition – is the quality of the people. So often in British industry we are prepared to accept second best. The Nissan view has been to identify very clearly the type of people we are seeking – and not compromise. It is better to delay appointment rather than appoint quickly and live to regret it. Critically, having determined the philosophy, we sought people with a good general engineering and/or production background (except for certain key jobs where specific auto manufacturing experience was necessary) but who also had our desired characteristics of teamworking, quality consciousness and flexibility. Only by establishing in advance the characteristics you are seeking will you be able to hire people who fit that pattern. This does not mean hiring clones, for when you are also looking for people who can make effective individual contributions, a wide variety of personalities is essential. To hire successfully, however, it must be recognised that the straight interview is the most unreliable of predictors. Thus all selection is based on various permutations of aptitude test, personality assessment, skills test, group discussion and interviews. Only by looking at people in different ways over several sessions is it possible to minimise the chances of making mistakes.

The results speak for themselves. Every indicator is better than anticipated. Quality standards exceed Nissan's world-wide target, schedules are always met, the commitment of all staff can, according to most visitors, virtually be felt, improvements in quality and productivity are constantly made by the people actually doing the job, turnover and absenteeism is low, lateness is virtually non-existent. Resulting partly from this the company has regularly announced plans to expand its Sunderland plant.

Importantly however the same pattern emerges from other companies which have gone down this road. There is nothing special to Japanese companies, greenfield sites, new technology or single union deals. There are sufficient companies in the UK to prove the success of this approach. Companies such as Nissan, IBM, Pilkington, Eaton, Nabisco, Whitbread, Continental, Formica, Eldridge Pope, Kimberley Clark, Hardy Spicer, Inmos, Norsk Hydro and many others have looked at the totality of the 'people' part of their business and in addition to mouthing the platitude 'People are our most important asset' are actually behaving that way. They have looked strategically at their human resources and have determined how to get from 'here' to 'there'. They have not imposed change but have taken people with them.

Critical among the groups that have to be involved are the first line supervisors. At grass roots level they are the people who, if not convinced, will ensure failure. To ask a group selected on the basis of their ability to handle technical problems and operate in an adversarial style to manage in a different way can give rise to many fears and suspicions, not least of which is a concern about their own capabilities. To someone brought up on the basis that the boss has the monopoly of wisdom, the concept of encouraging subordinates to come up with better ways can be somewhat frightening. Perhaps a guarantee that no one will lose their employment (albeit they may need to change jobs) because of a change in management approach will be helpful.

In the chapter discussing the future role of trade unions, the question was asked as to what role the trade union movement will have to play in a company which adopts this integrated approach. It is for the trade unions to answer this, but it is becoming increasingly difficult for management to argue that trade unions are an insuperable barrier to change. In the 1960s, trade unions were seen as Luddites opposing the introduction of 'new technology'. Today the vast majority have accepted and indeed welcome such innovation. What is needed is a management that is prepared to take the lead and then take the trade unions with it. Trade unions will succeed if they learn to adapt. Throughout their history the mainstream of trade unionism has, eventually, accepted change. While the pace of acceptance needs to be accelerated there is no doubt of the fact of acceptance.

One other factor that is important is the time span of success within which companies operate. In Japan it is not insignificant that the institutional shareholders also provide services to the individual companies. The insurance companies, for example, which are major shareholders, are also the companies through which insurance is placed. The Japanese are concerned with long-term survival and success of a group of people rather than short-term returns from the company in which they invest. It is easy in the UK to get all the costs of the integrated approach and few of the benefits – and it is the costs that the investor first sees.

This attitude affects not only the approach to human resources but all aspects of the business and results in British management being under greater short term pressure than many of its competitors. But while such pressures may make it more difficult for the British manager, it is no excuse for not trying. Those who do not seek to change – even those who are currently successful – will be the ones eventually to fail.

The essential factor making for success is not a greenfield site, new capital investment, or even a new man at the top. It is managers having the *perception* of what they wish to achieve and then the *will* to make it happen. As previously stated there is no magic formula but the people part of the business must be considered strategically and then fully integrated with the overall business plan.

Whatever the circumstances of a company, without the perception and the will nothing will change for the better!

Notes and References

Introduction: The View from Abroad

1. NEDO *Industrial Relations in Britain: an introduction for inward investors* (1979).
2. Department of Employment *Strikes in Britain* (HMSO, 1978).

1 'Them and Us' ... to just 'Us'

1. Charles Booth and others *Life and Labour of the People in London* (Macmillan 1902) (quoted in 'Staff Status for All' – IPM, 1977).
2. W.B. Pinkerton *William Cobbett* (Penguin, 1949) (quoted in 'Staff Status for All' – IPM, 1977).
3. C.E. Parsons 'Clerks, their position and advancement' 1876 (quoted in *Status and Benefits in Industry* (Industrial Society, 1966).
4. B.G. Orchard *The Clerks of Liverpool* (Collinson, 1871). (quoted in 'Staff Status for All', IPM, 1977).
5. G.S. Bain *The Growth of White Collar Unionism* (Oxford University Press, 1970).
6. T.U.C. *Employment and Technology* (1979).
7. *Code of Industrial Relations Practice* (HMSO, 1972).
8. *In Place of Strife* (HMSO, 1969).
9. J. Conway *AEU Journal* (1965).
10. H. Murlis and J. Grist *Towards single status* (BIM, 1976).
11. *Federation Statement on Harmonisation* (EEF, 1980).
12. R.D. Hulme and R.V. Bevan 'The blue collar worker goes on salary', *Harvard Business Review*, March–April 1975.
13. H. Gibson 'Common staff status in IBM', *Industrial Participation*, Winter 1979–80.
14. H. Murlis and J. Grist, *Towards single status*.
15. Ibid.
16. R.D. Hulme and R.V. Bevan 'The blue collar worker goes on salary'.

2 Japanese Management – Separating Reality from the Myth

1. *State of Operations of Japanese Affiliates (Manufacturing) in Europe* (Japan External Trade Organisation, 1985).
2. *Things you Want to Know about Nissan and Japan* (Nissan Motor Company Ltd).
3. Michio Morishima *Why has Japan Succeeded* (Cambridge University Press, 1982).
4. Marvin Wolf *The Japanese Conspiracy* (New English Library, 1985).
5. William Ouchi *Theory Z* (Addison Wesley Publishing Co., 1981).

6.   Dick Wilson *The Sun at Noon* (Hamish Hamilton, 1986).
7.   Keith Thurley 'A touch of genius or purely indigenous?', *Europe-Asia Business Review*, April 1984.
8.   *Yomiuri Shimbun* quoted in *Manpower Argus* (Manpower Temporary Services, May 1986).
9.   *Japan Economic Journal* quoted in *Manpower Argus* (Manpower Temporary Services, September 1986).
10.   *Labor Trends in Japan* (US Embassy, 1982) (quoted in M. Wolf op cit).
11.   Ian Gow 'Raiders, invaders or simply good traders', *Accounting*, March 1986.
12.   Dick Wilson *The Sun at Noon*.

3   Flexibility – the 1980s' Variety

1.   '*Craft flexibility*' Incomes Data Services Study No. 322, September 1984.
2.   'From craftsman to programmer', *AEU Journal*, June 1984.
3.   Robert Taylor 'The union no-strike force', *Management Today*, April 1985.
4.   *The Union for the Future* (EETPU, 1984).
5.   *Flexibility at Work*, Incomes Data Services Study No. 360, April 1986.
6.   Ibid.
7.   *Changing working patterns – how companies achieve flexibility to meet new needs*, Institute of Manpower Studies, NEDO 1986.
8.   'Flexibility – who needs it?', CAITS, Polytechnic of North London, 1986.

4   Numerical Flexibility – A Fashionable Theory

1.   Institute of Manpower Studies Survey, *Employment Gazette*, January 1986.
2.   John Atkinson 'Flexibility: planning for an uncertain future', *Manpower Policy and Practice*, Spring 1985.
3.   Roger Leek 'Flexible manning in practice: Control Data' *Manpower policy and practice*, Summer 1985.
4.   Quoted in *Financial Times*, 5 December 1986.

5   Quality – Above All

1.   Ian Gow 'Raiders, Invaders'.
2.   Ron Collard and Barrie Dale 'Quality Circles – why they break down and why they hold up', *Personnel Management*, February 1985.
3.   *Employee Involvement and Quality Circles* (TGWU).
4.   D. Wallace Bell 'Report on America', *Industrial Participation*, Summer 1985.

5. *Quality Control Circles* (Department of Trade and Industry, 1984).
6. Collard and Dale 'Quality Circles'.

6 Teamworking and Commitment – Philosophy and Practice

1. Max Weber *The Protestant Ethic and the Spirit of Capitalism* (Allen & Unwin, 1930).
2. A. E. Best 'Change – the blend of reality and vision', *Industrial Participation* No. 589, Winter 1985/86.
3. I. Robertson and M. Smith *Motivation and Job Design* (IPM 1985).
4. *Meeting the challenge of change*, Work Research Unit, June 1982.
5. Richard E. Walton 'From control to commitment in the workplace', *Harvard Business Review*, March 1985.
6. 'At the Four Year Mark: QWL at Detroit Gear and Axle', *World of Work* Report, February 1985.
7. 'Job 1 at Ford: Employee co-operation', *Employee Relations*, 1985.
8. *Bargaining Report 45*, Labour Research Department, 1985.
9. *Survey of Catering Costs, Prices and Subsidies* (Industrial Society, 1986).
10. *Volvo, Kalmar Revisited – ten years of experience* (Development Council of Sweden, 1984).
11. Walton 'From control to commitment'.

7 Commitment – Not Sickness – Determines Attendance

1. Brian Willey *Union Recognition and Representation in Engineering* (Engineering Employers Federation, 1986).
2. Manpower Paper No. 4 (Department of Employment 1973).
3. Dr P. Taylor 'Sickness absence: Facts and misconceptions', *Journal of the Royal College of Physicians*, July 1974.
4. *General Household Survey* (HMSO 1985).
5. *Private health insurance*, IDS Survey No. 317, July 1984.

8 Evaluation, Payment and Appraisal – Servants, not Masters

1. *Job Evaluation Review* (IDS Top Pay Unit, July 1983).
2. 'Job Evaluation', NBPI Report No. 83 (HMSO 1968).
3. *Job Evaluation and Changing Technology*, Work Research Unit Occasional Paper No. 23, 1982.
4. News and Abstracts No. 77, Work Research Unit, November–December 1985.
5. 'Merit pay for manual workers', *Industrial Relations Review and Reports No. 367*, May 1986.
6. 'Integrated job evaluation at Continental Can', *Industrial Relations Review and Reports No. 291*, March 1983.
7. IRRR, No. 291.

8. Quoted in *Progressive Payment Systems*, Work Research Unit Occasional Paper, February 1984.
9. Ibid.
10. *Industrial Relations Review and Reports No. 319*, May 1984.
11. *Progressive Payment Systems*.
12. *Performance Appraisal Revisited* (Institute of Personnel Management, 1986).

9 The Union Question

1. *Employment Gazette* (HMSO, January 1986).
2. Ian Linn *Single Unions Deals* (Northern College, 1986).
3. *Observer*, 28 April 1985.
4. 'No strike deals in perspective', *Industrial Relations Review and Reports No. 324*, July 1984.
5. See, for example, *The Sunday Times*, 29 December 1985.
6. Sir John Wood 'Last offer arbitration', *British Journal of Industrial Relations*, November 1985.
7. *Annual Report*, Central Arbitration Committee, 1985.
8. IDS Report *Collective Bargaining*.
9. *Industrial Relations Review and Reports No. 364*, March 1986.
10. Brian Willey 'Union recognition and representation'.
11. P. Garrahan – *Capital and Class*, Winter 1986.
12. 1986 Annual Report Advisory, Conciliation and Arbitration Service 1987.

10 Production Management – Enriching the Poor Relation

1. 'Attracting the brightest students into industry', *Opinion Research and Communication* (Committtee for Research into Public Attitudes, 1985).
2. *Supervisors of manual workers*, IDS Study No. 346, September 1985.
3. *Supervisors of manual workers*.
4. Soraya Romano 'How supervisors tamed the wild cat strikers', *Works Management*, September 1984.
5. Peter Saville *Psychological Testing in the 1980s* (Saville & Holdsworth Ltd, 1985).
6. Peter Hetherington in The *Guardian*.
7. 'Supervisors of manual workers'.
8. Paul Hill *Towards a New Philosophy of Management* (Gower Press, 1974).

Conclusion: Human Resources – a Strategy

1. As described by Thomas Furtado, Director, Employee, Communications, at the NEDC Conference 'Enterprise, Success and Jobs', 29 April 1987.

Index

Note: Throughout this index Nissan Motor Manufacturing (UK) Ltd is referred to as NMUK, and Continental Can Company (UK) Ltd as Continental.